Answer The Call - 31 Days of Biblical Action

Joshua Rhoades

Published by Joshua Paul Rhoades, 2024.

ANSWER THE CALL - 31 DAYS OF BIBLICAL ACTION

First edition. October 11, 2024.

ISBN: 979-8227737861

Written by Joshua Rhoades.

Also by Joshua Rhoades

Courage Under Fire: David's Stand On The Battlefield
Jonah's Journey: Voices Of Redemption And Lessons In Obedience
The Furnace Of Faith: 12 Principles From The Heat Of Faith
Whispers of Hope: Inspiring Stories of Men's Prayers In Scripture
Frontier Legends: The Oregon Dream
Elijah: A Beacon Of Boldness
HOOK, LINE & SAVIOUR - Faith Reflections from Fishing
Driven By Faith: Motor Racing Inspired Christian Life
30 Day Devotional - Bold and Strong- Coffee Devotions for a Courageous
Christian Walk
Authentic Christianity: The Heart of Old Time Religion
Consider The Ant - God's Tiny Preachers
Flee Fornication: The Plea For Purity
Renewed Hope- How to Find Encouragement in God
Sounding The Call - The Voice of Conviction
The Altar - Where Heaven Meets Earth
The Bible's Battlefields- Timeless Lessons from Ancient Wars
The Sacred Art of Silence - How Silence Speaks in Scripture
Under Fire- The Sanctity of the Traditional Biblical Home
Who Is on the Lord's Side? A Call to Righteousness
What Is Truth? - From Skepticism to Submission
First and Goal- Faith and Football Fundamentals
From Dugout to Devotion- Spiritual Lessons from Baseball
Par for the Course- Faith and Fairways
The Believer's Pace- Tools for Running Life's Marathon
The Immutable Fortress- Security in God's Unchanging Nature
Biblical Bravery
Deer Stands and Devotions: A Hunter's Walk with God

Jesus Knows- Our Hearts, Our Responsibility
Restoration - Setting The Bone
Spiritual 911- God's Word for Life's Emergency's
The Freedom of Forgiveness
The Jezebel Effect - Ancient Manipulations Modern Lessons
The Shout That Stopped The Saviour
The Time Machine Chronicles: Old Testament Characters
Anchored In Truth Exploring The Depths of Psalm 119
Biblical Counsel on Anger
Proverbs' Portraits The Men God Mentions
Stumbling in the Dark - The Dangers of Alcohol
Guarding the Wicket Protecting Your Faith and Game
The Champion's Faith - Wrestling and Achieving Spiritual Victory
Scriptural Commands for Modern Times Living God's Word Today Volume 1
Scriptural Commands for Modern Times Living God's Word Today Volume 2
Scriptural Commands for Modern Times Living God's Word TodayVolume3
The Greatest Gift
A Christmas Journey of Faith
Daughter Of The King: Embracing Your Identity In Christ
Determination and Dedication Building Strong Faith As A Young Man
Walking Through Walls God's Power to Part the Storms of Life
David's Song Of Deliverance Praising God Through Every Storm
From Weakness to Warrior: Gideon's Transformation
Why Did Jesus Weep?
Living For God The Call To Be A Living Sacrifice
My Mind Is In A Fog What Do I Do?
Turning The Page Written By Grace
The Calling and Greatness of John the Baptist
For Such a Time Esther's Courageous Stand
From Brokenness To Beauty Written By The Pen of Grace
The Ultimate Guide to Massive Action- From Plans to Reality
A Heart Of Conviction
Serving In The Shadows
Repentance Revealed The Road Back To God
The Chief Sinner Meets The Chief Saviour Reflections On I Timothy 1:15

Dedication

To you, the reader of "Answer the Call – 31 Days of Biblical Action" , this book is dedicated with a heart full of gratitude and hope. You hold in your hands not just words on a page, but an invitation to embark on a life-changing journey—one that calls you to deepen your faith, embrace God's plan for your life, and act boldly on the teachings of Scripture.

As you walk through these next 31 days, I want you to know how valued you are in this process. Every step you take, every action you commit to, is significant in the eyes of God. Whether you are coming to this devotional as a seasoned believer seeking fresh inspiration or as someone newly exploring faith, I believe that the Holy Spirit has brought you here for a reason. You are not reading this by accident. You are here, ready to answer the call that God has placed uniquely on your life.

Each day, as you encounter a new action verb, remember that the same God who breathed life into Scripture is walking with you through every moment. The actions you will be called to—whether it's to love, forgive, serve, trust, or pray—are not only meant to transform you but also to impact the lives of those around you. You are part of something greater. Your response to God's call matters, and it carries the power to bring light and hope into the world.

There will be moments when the call may seem challenging. You may be asked to step out of your comfort zone, to stretch your faith in ways you haven't before. In those moments, I encourage you to lean into God's strength. Know that you are not alone. The God who calls you will also equip you with everything you need to fulfill His purpose. You are capable of more than you realize because God is working in and through you.

As you dedicate these next 31 days to pursuing biblical action, be kind to yourself. Some days will feel easier than others, and that's okay. What matters most is that you continue moving forward, one step at a time, trusting that God is guiding your path. Each day is an opportunity to grow closer to Him, to reflect His love in new ways, and to live out your faith with courage and conviction.

I am excited for you, and I am praying for you as you begin this journey. May this devotional not only inspire you but also empower you to live a life that fully answers the call of Christ. May you experience His peace, joy, and strength in every moment. And may you come to the end of these 31 days transformed, renewed, and ready to continue walking in faith with a heart set on action.

You are called, chosen, and deeply loved. Now is the time to "Answer the Call".

Introduction

In "Answer the Call – 31 Days of Bold Biblical Action", you are invited on a transformative journey through 31 powerful verbs from Scripture—each one a call to action that challenges you to step out in faith, live boldly for God, and deepen your walk with Christ. Every word from the Bible is packed with meaning, but the verbs—the action words—are what ignite our faith, push us forward, and invite us to live out the truth of God's Word in our everyday lives. Over the next 31 days, you will be encouraged to answer God's call in specific, practical ways that align with these biblical verbs, one for each day. Whether it's seek, pray, love, forgive, or rejoice, each verb holds a vital command, a way to live more fully in God's purpose. This book is not just about reading Scripture—it's about doing it. As James 1:22 says, "But be ye doers of the word, and not hearers only, deceiving your own selves."

The verbs of Scripture are not passive suggestions; they are bold invitations into an active relationship with God. These 31 days are designed to take you from simply knowing about God's commands to living them out in ways that can transform your heart, your relationships, and your community. When you seek God first, you align your priorities with His kingdom. When you love your neighbor as yourself, you step into a world that desperately needs the love of Christ. When you pray without ceasing, you cultivate a life dependent on the power of God. Each verb is an opportunity to draw nearer to God and to impact the world around you for His glory.

This journey is not about perfection—it's about progress. As you commit to answering the call of one verb each day, you'll experience the challenge of faith in action, but you'll also experience the joy and peace that comes from obeying God. You'll find that each verb, though simple, contains layers of meaning that go far beyond the surface. For instance, when Jesus says, "Come unto me, all *ye* that labour and are heavy laden, and I will give you rest" (Matthew 11:28),

He is inviting you into a deeper relationship with Him. That single word, come, is not just about physical movement—it's a spiritual call to trust, to surrender your burdens, and to receive His rest.

Likewise, verbs like rejoice and give thanks remind us that gratitude and joy are choices we make daily, regardless of our circumstances. These actions shift our focus from our struggles to the goodness of God, transforming our hearts and renewing our minds. Verbs like forgive call us to let go of bitterness and extend grace, just as Christ has forgiven us. Each day's verb brings its own challenge, but it also brings a promise—when we step out in obedience, God meets us with His grace, His strength, and His peace.

As you embark on this journey through "Answer the Call – 31 Days of Bold Biblical Action", prepare your heart to be stretched, encouraged, and transformed. This book is not a passive devotional, but a roadmap for living out the vibrant, active faith that God calls us to. You'll find that the power of these verbs doesn't come from human effort alone, but from the Holy Spirit working in and through you. As you respond to each call with faith and courage, you will experience God's faithfulness in new and deeper ways. Whether you are a new believer or have been walking with Christ for years, this book will challenge you to go further, to dig deeper, and to live out your faith with boldness.

The next 31 days are an invitation to step into the fullness of the life God has for you. Every day presents an opportunity to take a bold step of faith, to act on the words of Scripture, and to see God's power at work in your life. Will you answer the call? Will you take the verbs of Scripture and make them your daily actions? As you say yes to this challenge, you'll find that your faith grows stronger, your love for others deepens, and your relationship with God becomes richer than you ever imagined. Get ready to answer the call, and to experience the joy, peace, and power that come from living out God's Word one action at a time.

Chapter 1 – Seek

In the first call to action from "Answer the Call – 31 Days of Bold Biblical Action", we are invited to focus on one of the most profound and challenging commands from Jesus: to seek first the kingdom of God and His righteousness. In Matthew 6:33, Jesus speaks directly to our hearts, calling us to align our priorities with His divine plan. "But seek ye first the kingdom of God, and his righteousness; and all these things shall be added unto you." He says, urging us to center our lives around Him and the values of His kingdom. This is not just a gentle suggestion or a hopeful ideal—it's a bold directive that demands our attention and commitment. To seek the kingdom of God first means to make it the highest priority in our lives, above all other pursuits, desires, and distractions. It is a call to shift our focus from the temporary things of this world to the eternal things of God. But how do we truly seek the kingdom of God in a world that constantly pulls us in different directions, and what does it mean to seek His righteousness? This journey begins with a wholehearted pursuit of God and His will, but it continues through daily surrender, faith, and action.

Jesus' words in Matthew 6:33 come in the context of His famous Sermon on the Mount, where He addresses the worries and anxieties that weigh on the hearts of His listeners. He speaks to the universal concerns that we all have—about food, clothing, shelter, and the future. These are legitimate needs, and Jesus knows that we care deeply about them. However, His challenge to us is this: don't let those worries consume you. Instead, let your primary concern be the kingdom of God. When you seek first God's kingdom, He promises to provide for your needs. But what does it mean to seek the kingdom? It means to pursue God's reign and rule in every aspect of our lives. It means allowing His principles, His values, and His commands to govern our decisions, our relationships, our work, and our hearts. Seeking the kingdom isn't just about looking forward to heaven someday—it's about bringing God's presence and His ways into our everyday lives here and now.

At its core, seeking the kingdom of God is about seeking a relationship with the King. It's not just about religious duty or good deeds; it's about knowing God intimately and letting that relationship shape everything we do. To seek first the kingdom is to put God at the center of our lives—to make Him the foundation upon which everything else is built. It means making time for Him, spending time in prayer, studying His Word, and allowing His Spirit to transform our hearts and minds. It's about letting God's priorities become our priorities, and His desires become our desires. This kind of seeking requires intentionality. It doesn't happen by accident, and it doesn't come from simply going through the motions of faith. It requires a daily decision to put God first, to make Him the most important pursuit in our lives. When we seek God in this way, we begin to see the world through His eyes, and we start to live in a way that reflects His love, His justice, and His truth.

But Jesus doesn't stop at telling us to seek the kingdom of God. He also calls us to seek His righteousness. Righteousness, in this context, means living in a way that is aligned with God's character and His standards. It's about living rightly—choosing to live in obedience to God's commands and reflecting His holiness in our actions, words, and attitudes. To seek God's righteousness means to desire what is right according to God's standards, not according to the world's. It means pursuing purity, justice, kindness, and love in all that we do. But seeking righteousness is not about trying to be perfect in our own strength. It's about relying on God's grace and the power of the Holy Spirit to help us live in a way that honors Him. As we seek His righteousness, we grow in our understanding of what it means to live as citizens of His kingdom, and we begin to reflect His character more and more in our daily lives.

To seek first the kingdom of God and His righteousness is a radical call. It's a call to surrender everything—our plans, our desires, our worries, and our control—and trust that God's ways are higher than our ways. It's a call to live counter-culturally, to resist the pull of the world that tells us to seek after wealth, success, power, or comfort above all else. Instead, we are called to seek after God, trusting that He will provide for our needs and guide us on the path that leads to true fulfillment and peace. This kind of seeking requires faith. It means trusting that God is good, that He knows what we need, and that His plans for us are better than anything we could plan for ourselves. It's about believing that when we put God first, everything else will fall into place, even if it doesn't always look the way we expect.

The challenge of seeking the kingdom first is that it demands a shift in our priorities. It asks us to examine what we truly value and what we are pursuing with our time, energy, and resources. Are we seeking God above all else, or are we allowing other things to take His place? It's easy to get caught up in the busyness of life, in the pursuit of career goals, financial stability, or personal achievements. These things aren't inherently wrong, but Jesus reminds us that they should never come before our pursuit of Him. When we seek first the kingdom, we are trusting that God will take care of the rest. We are releasing our need to control every outcome and trusting that God's provision is enough. This doesn't mean that we stop working hard or being responsible, but it does mean that we stop worrying and striving in our own strength. Instead, we place our lives, our future, and our trust in God's hands.

The promise that comes with seeking the kingdom first is one of provision. Jesus assures us that when we make God our priority, "all these things" will be added unto us. He knows our needs better than we do, and He promises to meet them when we put Him first. But this promise is not a guarantee of material wealth or worldly success. Instead, it's a promise that God will give us exactly what we need—spiritually, emotionally, and physically—to fulfill His purpose for our lives. When we seek first the kingdom, we are no longer chasing after temporary things that fade away. Instead, we are investing in eternal treasures, building a life that is rooted in God's love and purpose.

As you begin this journey through "Answer the Call – 31 Days of Bold Biblical Action", let the call to "Seek ye first the kingdom of God, and his righteousness" be the foundation of everything you do. Let this be the day you decide to put God first in every area of your life. Allow Him to shape your priorities, guide your steps, and transform your heart. As you seek Him, you will discover that He is faithful to provide, to lead, and to use you in ways you never imagined. You will find that the kingdom of God is not just something to look forward to in the future—it is something to experience here and now, as you live in His presence and follow His will. Seek Him boldly, with all your heart, and watch as He brings His kingdom to life in and through you.

Chapter 2 – Ask

In the second call to action from "Answer the Call – 31 Days of Bold Biblical Action", we are invited to consider one of the most powerful promises Jesus gave His followers: "Ask, and it shall be given you" (Matthew 7:7). These simple yet profound words hold the key to experiencing the fullness of God's blessings and guidance in our lives. To ask is to approach God with a heart of faith, trust, and expectation, believing that He not only hears our prayers but delights in answering them. This call to ask is not a timid or half-hearted request—it's a bold invitation to bring our needs, desires, and hopes before the throne of God, trusting that He is both willing and able to provide for us. Yet, there is more to this promise than simply making requests. Jesus' instruction to "ask" challenges us to deepen our relationship with Him, to lean into our dependence on God, and to trust in His timing and wisdom in ways we may not always fully understand. It's a call to recognize that God is a loving Father who desires to give good gifts to His children, and it's a call to bold, persistent prayer that stretches our faith and deepens our connection with Him.

At its core, this verse from Matthew 7:7 is an invitation to intimacy with God. Asking implies a relationship; you don't ask things of someone you don't trust or have confidence in. Jesus is reminding us that we are invited into a relationship with our heavenly Father where we can bring our deepest needs, our greatest desires, and even our smallest concerns to Him, knowing that He cares for us. The act of asking God for what we need or want is not about treating Him like a vending machine or only coming to Him when we're in trouble. It's about living in constant communication with Him, recognizing that He is the source of everything good in our lives. It's about humbly admitting that we are not self-sufficient and that we need God's help, provision, and guidance in every area of our lives. To ask, in this sense, is to open our hearts to God, to rely on His goodness, and to trust that He will respond in ways that are best for us.

But asking requires faith. When Jesus says, "Ask, and it shall be given you," He is calling us to ask with the expectation that God will answer. This doesn't mean we will always get exactly what we ask for or that God is obligated to give us whatever we want. Rather, it means that when we ask in faith, believing in God's goodness and sovereignty, we can trust that He will give us what we need according to His perfect will. This kind of faith isn't about manipulating God into doing what we want, but about aligning our hearts with His will and trusting that He knows what is best. It's about asking with the confidence that God is always working for our good, even when His answers come in ways we didn't expect. Sometimes God's answers come quickly, and other times they come after a season of waiting. Sometimes God says "yes," and other times He says "no" or "not yet." But in every situation, His response is rooted in love and wisdom, and we can trust that He will always do what is best for us.

Jesus' call to ask also speaks to the importance of persistence in prayer. In the verses that follow Matthew 7:7, Jesus goes on to say, "For everyone who asks receives; the one who seeks finds; and to the one who knocks, the door will be opened." The imagery of knocking and seeking suggests a kind of prayer that is not passive, but active and persistent. It's not about asking once and then giving up if we don't see immediate results. It's about continuing to ask, continuing to knock, and continuing to seek, knowing that God honors perseverance. Jesus is teaching us that we are not meant to give up easily when it comes to prayer. We are called to keep asking, keep seeking, and keep knocking, trusting that God will answer in His perfect timing. This kind of persistence stretches our faith and deepens our trust in God, because it forces us to rely on Him even when we don't see immediate answers. It teaches us to wait on the Lord, to trust His timing, and to believe that He is always working, even when we don't see it.

One of the most powerful aspects of asking is that it reminds us of our dependence on God. So often, we try to handle life's challenges on our own. We make plans, set goals, and try to solve problems in our own strength. But when we stop and ask God for help, we are acknowledging that we can't do it on our own. We are admitting that we need His guidance, His provision, and His power to accomplish anything of lasting value. Asking humbles us because it reminds us that we are not in control—God is. It reminds us that everything we have comes from Him, and that apart from Him, we can do nothing. This humility is the foundation of a healthy, vibrant relationship with God. When we ask, we are not only opening ourselves up to receiving God's blessings, but we are also deepening our dependence on Him and learning to trust Him more fully.

Jesus' command to ask is also an invitation to experience God's goodness. When we ask, we are not coming before a distant or indifferent deity—we are coming before a loving Father who delights in giving good gifts to His children. Jesus Himself goes on to say in Matthew 7:9-11, "Which of you, if your son asks for bread, will give him a stone? Or if he asks for a fish, will give him a snake? If you then, though you are evil, know how to give good gifts to your children, how much more will your Father in heaven give good gifts to those who ask Him!" God's heart toward us is one of generosity and love. He wants to bless us, guide us, and provide for our needs. But He also wants us to come to Him, to ask Him, and to trust Him to provide. Asking is not just about receiving things from God—it's about experiencing His goodness, His love, and His care in a personal and tangible way.

But asking requires vulnerability. It requires us to admit our need and to trust that God will meet that need in His way and in His time. This can be difficult, especially if we've been disappointed in the past or if we're afraid that God won't answer in the way we hope. But Jesus' words in Matthew 7:7 are a promise—when we ask, it will be given to us. This doesn't mean that God will give us everything we ask for exactly as we ask for it, but it does mean that God will always answer in the way that is best for us. Sometimes that answer is "yes," sometimes it's "no," and sometimes it's "wait." But in every case, God's answer is a reflection of His love and His perfect wisdom. Asking requires us to trust that God knows what we need better than we do, and that His answers are always for our good.

As you continue through "Answer the Call – 31 Days of Bold Biblical Action", let this call to ask be a reminder of the incredible privilege we have to come before God with our needs, desires, and concerns. Let it be a challenge to deepen your faith and your relationship with Him by asking boldly, persistently, and with great expectation. Don't be afraid to ask God for big things, because He is a big God who is able to do far more than we could ever ask or imagine. But also be willing to trust Him when His answers don't look like what you expected. Trust that He is good, that He loves you, and that He is always working for your good, even when you don't see it.

Ask with boldness. Ask with faith. Ask with persistence. And trust that your Father in heaven hears you, loves you, and will answer you in His perfect time and way. When we ask, we are not just making requests—we are drawing closer to the heart of God, learning to trust Him more deeply, and opening ourselves up to the fullness of His blessings and His will for our lives. So ask, and it shall be given to you. Seek, and you will find. Knock, and the door will be opened to you. And as you ask, watch as God responds with love, grace, and power, revealing His goodness and faithfulness in ways you never imagined.

Chapter 3 – Knock

In the third call to action from "Answer the Call – 31 Days of Bold Biblical Action", Jesus invites us to take a bold step of faith with His simple yet powerful instruction: "Ask, and it shall be given you; seek, and ye shall find; knock, and it shall be opened unto you:" (Matthew 7:7). These words are filled with deep meaning and challenge us to live with perseverance, determination, and trust in God's faithfulness. To knock is to seek access, to reach out in hope, and to expect something beyond the door. It is an active, deliberate choice to pursue what God has for us, believing that He stands ready to open doors that lead to deeper understanding, spiritual growth, and opportunities we might have never imagined. Knocking is not a passive act; it's a declaration of faith. It's an expression of belief that God is on the other side, waiting to open the door when we come to Him. But what does it mean to truly knock? It means more than simply standing at the door and waiting—it requires persistence, a spirit that refuses to give up, and a heart that believes the door will be opened because God has promised it will.

To knock is to approach God with a heart full of expectation, knowing that He is both willing and able to respond. Jesus' words encourage us to knock with confidence, trusting that God is always ready to hear us, to respond to our cries, and to open doors of opportunity, healing, restoration, or guidance. This call to knock challenges us to be bold in our pursuit of God, to come before Him with our requests, desires, and questions, knowing that He welcomes us with open arms. Knocking implies that there is something on the other side—a promise, an answer, a breakthrough—that God wants us to access, but it also requires that we take the initiative to ask for it. In other words, knocking is an invitation to press into God's presence with faith, persistence, and hope, believing that He will respond in His perfect timing.

But knocking isn't always easy. Sometimes, we knock on doors that seem to remain closed for a long time. We pray, we ask, we seek, and yet it feels like nothing is happening. In these moments, it can be tempting to stop knocking, to give up, or to assume that maybe God isn't listening. But Jesus tells us to keep knocking. This call to action is not about knocking once and then walking away if the door doesn't immediately open. It's about persistence—it's about knocking with the expectation that God will answer, even if it takes time. Jesus calls us to a life of persistent prayer, where we continue to knock on the door of heaven, trusting that God hears every single knock and will open the door at the right moment. This kind of persistence builds our faith. It teaches us to rely on God's timing rather than our own, to trust that He knows what's best for us, and to keep believing even when we can't see what's happening behind the scenes.

In the act of knocking, we are expressing our deep desire to see God move in our lives. We knock because we long for more of Him, more of His presence, more of His wisdom, and more of His direction. When we knock, we are asking for doors of opportunity to open, for doors of healing to be unlocked, for new beginnings to emerge. We knock because we know that without God's intervention, we can't move forward. And when we knock, we are trusting that God is on the other side, waiting to let us in. There is a sense of humility in knocking, because it requires us to admit that we cannot open the door ourselves. We need God to open it for us. Knocking is an act of faith that acknowledges our dependence on God and our willingness to trust Him to provide what we need.

The promise that comes with knocking is clear: the door will be opened. This is a guarantee from Jesus Himself. When we knock, we are not knocking on a door that will remain forever closed. God is not a distant figure who hides behind a door, refusing to answer. He is a loving Father who delights in opening doors for His children. However, the timing and the way in which God opens the door may not always match our expectations. Sometimes, God opens the door right away, and other times, He asks us to wait. Sometimes, He opens a door to something we didn't even realize we needed, and other times, He closes one door to open another. But the promise remains: when we knock, God will respond. Our job is to trust Him and keep knocking, knowing that His timing is perfect and His ways are higher than ours.

Knocking also represents perseverance. There are moments in life when we are faced with challenges, obstacles, or closed doors that seem impossible to overcome. In these moments, Jesus calls us to keep knocking. When we face difficult circumstances, when it feels like the doors to our dreams or our prayers are locked tight, we are called to persevere in faith. Knocking means not giving up, even when it feels hard. It means continuing to trust that God is working behind the scenes, preparing to open the door at just the right time. This kind of perseverance is built on the foundation of faith—it's a belief that God is faithful to His promises and that, in His time, He will open the door. Paul reminds us in Galatians 6:9, "Let us not become weary in doing good, for at the proper time we will reap a harvest if we do not give up." Knocking is an act of faith that refuses to give up, even when the answer doesn't come immediately.

When Jesus tells us to knock, He is inviting us into a deeper relationship with Him. He's inviting us to trust Him more fully, to seek Him more persistently, and to rely on His faithfulness. Knocking is not just about asking for what we want—it's about aligning our hearts with God's will and trusting that whatever door He opens will be for our good. Sometimes, we knock on doors that aren't meant to be opened, and in His wisdom, God gently redirects us to another door. Other times, we knock and find that the door leads to a path we didn't expect but one that is ultimately better than what we had imagined. The act of knocking is an act of surrender, where we lay down our own plans and desires and trust that God's plans are better.

In "Answer the Call – 31 Days of Bold Biblical Action", the call to knock is a call to live a life of faith-filled persistence. It's a call to keep praying, keep seeking, and keep believing that God is working, even when the doors seem closed. It's a challenge to not give up too soon, to not lose heart, but to trust that God is faithful to His word. The act of knocking is not just about opening physical doors—it's about opening spiritual doors as well. When we knock, we are asking God to open doors of understanding, to reveal His will for our lives, and to guide us into deeper relationship with Him. Knocking is about "But seek ye first the kingdom of God, and his righteousness; and all these things shall be added unto you." (Matthew 6:33).

As you continue through "Answer the Call – 31 Days of Bold Biblical Action", let this challenge to knock be a reminder that God is always near, always listening, and always ready to respond to His children. Whether you are knocking on the door of opportunity, healing, provision, or direction, know that God is faithful. He is not a God who withholds good things from His children—He is a God who delights in opening doors and inviting us into His presence. So, keep knocking. Keep seeking. Keep trusting that the door will be opened, even if it's not in the way or the timing you expect. God's promises are true, and His faithfulness endures through every season.

Knock with faith, knock with perseverance, and knock with the expectation that God will open the door at just the right time. He sees your heart, He hears your prayers, and He is ready to lead you into the plans and purposes He has prepared for you. The doors He opens will lead you to deeper joy, greater peace, and a closer walk with Him. So, knock, and it shall be opened to you.

Chapter 4 – Pray

In the fourth call to action from "Answer the Call – 31 Days of Bold Biblical Action", we are faced with one of the most powerful and challenging instructions in the Bible: "Pray without ceasing" (1 Thessalonians 5:17). These three words carry a deep, life-altering invitation that calls us to live in constant communion with God, to let prayer become the very heartbeat of our daily existence. But what does it mean to pray without ceasing? It doesn't mean spending every single moment in a formal prayer position or never leaving the quiet solitude of prayer. Instead, it's a call to a life that is so connected to God, so in tune with His presence, that we live in a continual state of conversation with Him. It's about an ongoing relationship where prayer becomes as natural as breathing, a constant dialogue with our Creator in every situation, in every emotion, and in every action. To pray without ceasing is to keep our hearts open to God, to invite Him into every corner of our lives, and to walk through each moment knowing that He is with us, listening, guiding, and responding.

This call to pray without ceasing invites us into a deeper, richer, more intimate relationship with God. It's not about reciting long, formal prayers or only seeking God when we are in need—it's about letting prayer become the rhythm of our lives. Just as we breathe in and out without thinking about it, prayer should become the natural response of our hearts. When we wake up in the morning, our first thought should be directed toward God, thanking Him for another day. As we go about our daily tasks—whether we're at work, at home, or running errands—we should keep that line of communication open, whispering prayers of gratitude, asking for wisdom, or seeking His guidance in every decision. When we face challenges, prayer should be our immediate response, turning to God in the moment of need rather than trying to handle things on our own. And when we experience joy and success, prayer should overflow from our hearts as we give thanks to the One who provides every good thing. In every season and circumstance, prayer should be the anchor that keeps us grounded in God's love and presence.

Praying without ceasing doesn't mean we are constantly on our knees or with our heads bowed, but it means that our hearts are always attuned to God. It's about living in an ongoing awareness of His presence, where we are constantly inviting Him into the everyday moments of our lives. Whether we're driving in the car, sitting at our desk, cooking dinner, or spending time with loved ones, we can pray. It's about having a mindset that seeks God in all things, big and small, and being open to His voice at any moment. Praying without ceasing is about making God the center of our lives, where everything we do is done in conversation with Him. It's about developing a habit of turning our thoughts toward God throughout the day, not just in times of crisis or need, but in times of joy, peace, and contentment as well. It's living with the constant awareness that God is near, that He cares about every detail of our lives, and that He is ready to listen whenever we speak.

One of the most beautiful aspects of praying without ceasing is that it transforms how we see the world. When we live in constant communication with God, we begin to see everything through the lens of His presence. Our problems don't seem as overwhelming when we know that God is with us, helping us carry the load. Our joys are sweeter when we share them with the One who gives us every blessing. Our decisions become clearer when we seek His wisdom at every turn. When we pray without ceasing, we are inviting God into every moment, allowing Him to shape our thoughts, guide our actions, and fill our hearts with His peace. This kind of prayer changes us from the inside out. It shifts our focus from ourselves and our worries to God and His goodness. It reminds us that we are never alone, that God is always with us, and that He is working in every situation, even when we can't see it.

Praying without ceasing also builds our faith. The more we pray, the more we see God's faithfulness in our lives. When we bring our needs and concerns to Him regularly, we begin to notice how He answers our prayers—sometimes in ways we expected, and other times in ways that surprise us. Prayer strengthens our relationship with God because it teaches us to rely on Him, to trust Him, and to expect Him to move in our lives. When we live in constant communication with God, we become more aware of His presence, and that awareness fuels our faith. We start to see God's fingerprints all around us—in the big moments and the small ones—and we are reminded that He is always at work, even when we don't realize it. Praying without ceasing reminds us that God is not distant or uninterested in our lives; He is near, He is listening, and He cares about every detail.

This call to pray without ceasing is also a reminder of our dependence on God. It's easy to go through life relying on our own strength, thinking we can handle things on our own. But when we live in constant prayer, we are reminded that we need God every moment of every day. Prayer keeps us humble because it acknowledges our need for God's help, wisdom, and guidance. It reminds us that we are not in control, but that God is—and that is a comforting truth. Praying without ceasing is about surrendering our need for control and trusting that God's plans are better than our own. It's about coming to Him with open hands, ready to receive whatever He has for us, knowing that His ways are higher than our ways and that He knows what is best for us.

Living a life of unceasing prayer also transforms our relationships with others. When we pray continually, we begin to see people through God's eyes. We become more compassionate, more patient, and more loving because we are constantly asking God to help us love others the way He loves us. Praying without ceasing means that we are not just praying for our own needs, but we are also praying for the people around us—our family, our friends, our co-workers, and even strangers we encounter throughout the day. Prayer opens our hearts to the needs of others and prompts us to intercede on their behalf. When we live in constant prayer, we become more sensitive to the needs of those around us, and we are more likely to reach out with kindness, encouragement, and support. Prayer shapes our hearts to be more like Christ's, and as we pray for others, we become vessels of His love and grace in the world.

But praying without ceasing is not just about talking to God—it's also about listening. True prayer is a two-way conversation, where we not only bring our requests to God, but we also take time to listen for His voice. When we live in constant prayer, we develop a sensitivity to the Holy Spirit's leading. We become more aware of His promptings, His guidance, and His comfort. Listening to God in prayer requires stillness, patience, and a willingness to hear what He has to say, even when it's not what we expect. Praying without ceasing means creating space in our hearts and minds to hear God's voice throughout the day, to be open to His direction, and to follow His leading wherever it may take us. It's about being attentive to the ways God is speaking to us, whether through His Word, through other people, or through the quiet whispers of His Spirit in our hearts.

As you continue through "Answer the Call – 31 Days of Bold Biblical Action", let this call to pray without ceasing be an invitation to deepen your relationship with God in new and powerful ways. Let it be a reminder that prayer is not just something we do occasionally or only in times of crisis—it's a way of life. It's an invitation to live in constant communion with God, to make prayer the foundation of everything we do, and to trust that He is always near, always listening, and always ready to respond. When we pray without ceasing, we are aligning our hearts with God's heart, allowing Him to transform us, guide us, and use us for His purposes.

This call to pray without ceasing is not a burden—it's a gift. It's an invitation to live in the freedom and joy of knowing that we are never alone, that we can talk to God at any time, and that He is always ready to listen. It's a call to live with a constant awareness of God's presence, to invite Him into every moment, and to trust that He is working in every situation. So, pray without ceasing. Talk to God throughout your day. Bring Him your worries, your joys, your questions, and your hopes. And listen for His voice, knowing that He is always speaking, always guiding, and always working for your good. When you live a life of unceasing prayer, you will experience the peace, joy, and strength that comes from walking closely with God every moment of every day.

Chapter 5 – Love

In the fifth call to action from "Answer the Call – 31 Days of Bold Biblical Action", we encounter one of the most profound and challenging commands Jesus ever gave: "And the second *is* like unto it, Thou shalt love thy neighbour as thyself." (Matthew 22:39). These words are simple yet carry a weight that can transform the way we live, the way we see the world, and the way we relate to others. To love our neighbor as ourselves is not just about being kind or polite—it's a radical, selfless, and sacrificial love that mirrors the love God has for us. Jesus places this command right alongside the greatest commandment to love God with all our heart, soul, and mind, showing that love for God and love for others are inseparable. When we truly love God, that love must overflow into how we treat others, because every person is made in His image. Loving our neighbor as ourselves is a call to step out of our comfort zones, to lay down our pride, and to see every person—whether friend, stranger, or enemy—with the same compassion, dignity, and care that we give to ourselves. It's not just an emotional feeling, but a choice to actively love in practical, real ways, even when it's hard, inconvenient, or undeserved.

Jesus' call to love our neighbor is a direct reflection of God's own character. God is love, and everything He does flows from His perfect love for humanity. When we love others, we are reflecting God's heart and participating in His work in the world. This kind of love goes beyond cultural expectations or human standards—it's a love that is unconditional, sacrificial, and all-encompassing. It's the same love that Jesus demonstrated when He laid down His life for us on the cross. To love our neighbor as ourselves means to put others' needs on the same level as our own, to consider their well-being with the same seriousness as we consider our own. It means treating others with the same kindness, patience, and grace that we would want to receive. But this isn't easy. Loving others as ourselves requires humility, selflessness, and a willingness to put aside our own desires and preferences for the sake of someone else. It means loving not just when it's convenient, but even when it's costly.

This command challenges us to examine how we view and treat those around us. Who is our neighbor? In the parable of the Good Samaritan, Jesus answers this question by showing that our neighbor is anyone in need, anyone we come across in our daily lives—whether they are like us or completely different from us. It's not just the people we are naturally close to or who are easy to love; it's also those who are difficult to love, those who may have hurt us, or those who live on the fringes of society. Our neighbor is the person we pass by on the street, the colleague who frustrates us, the family member we've been avoiding, and even the stranger we may never see again. Jesus calls us to love them all. This love is not dependent on whether the person "deserves" it or how they have treated us in the past. It's a love that transcends boundaries, expectations, and conditions. It's the kind of love that Jesus showed us—a love that reaches out to the broken, the lost, the difficult, and the unlovable.

To love our neighbor as ourselves also means recognizing that we are all deeply connected. What affects one person affects us all, and we are called to bear one another's burdens, to rejoice with those who rejoice, and to weep with those who weep. This command calls us to be compassionate, to see the world through the eyes of others, and to care about the struggles and joys of those around us. It means being willing to step into someone else's pain, to offer help when it's needed, and to stand up for justice when we see wrong being done. This kind of love is not passive—it's active, intentional, and sometimes messy. It involves getting involved in the lives of others, being present for them, and offering our time, resources, and hearts to meet their needs. It means going beyond surface-level niceties and being willing to truly walk alongside others, sharing in their burdens and joys.

But loving others as ourselves also requires us to love ourselves in the right way. This doesn't mean being selfish or self-centered, but it does mean recognizing our own worth as individuals created in the image of God. It means understanding that we are loved by God and that His love for us gives us the capacity to love others. When we grasp the depth of God's love for us—His forgiveness, His grace, and His compassion—it transforms the way we see ourselves and, in turn, the way we love others. We cannot truly love others in the way Jesus commands until we have first received and embraced God's love for us. When we love ourselves in the light of God's love, we are free to love others without seeking anything in return, because we know that our worth is not based on how others treat us, but on how God sees us.

This command to love our neighbor as ourselves also speaks to the importance of forgiveness. We live in a broken world where people hurt one another, where relationships are strained, and where forgiveness can be incredibly difficult. But Jesus calls us to forgive, just as we have been forgiven. Loving our neighbor means being willing to let go of bitterness, resentment, and the desire for revenge. It means choosing to extend grace, even when it's hard, because we have received grace ourselves. Forgiveness is one of the highest expressions of love, and when we forgive, we are reflecting the heart of God. To love as Jesus loves means to offer forgiveness freely, without conditions, and to seek reconciliation whenever possible. This doesn't mean ignoring the pain or pretending that hurt didn't happen, but it does mean releasing the burden of unforgiveness and trusting God to heal and restore.

Loving our neighbor as ourselves also calls us to live with a spirit of generosity. It's about being willing to share what we have—our time, our resources, our energy—with those who need it. It's about living with open hands, ready to give to others as freely as God has given to us. This kind of love is not about keeping track of what we've given or expecting something in return—it's about giving out of the overflow of God's love in our hearts. Whether it's offering a listening ear, providing for someone's physical needs, or simply being present in someone's life, loving others requires us to be generous with our lives. When we live generously, we are reflecting the generous heart of God, who gave us everything when He gave us His Son.

Jesus' command to love our neighbor as ourselves also calls us to stand up for justice. It's about caring for the marginalized, the oppressed, and the overlooked. Throughout Scripture, we see God's heart for justice and His call for His people to defend the rights of the poor and the needy, to speak up for those who cannot speak for themselves, and to act justly in all we do. To love our neighbor means to care about the injustices that affect others and to be willing to do something about it. It means advocating for those who are hurting, working to right the wrongs we see, and using our voices to bring about change. This kind of love is not passive—it's active and courageous, and it reflects the heart of a God who is always on the side of the oppressed and the brokenhearted.

Ultimately, Jesus' call to love our neighbor as ourselves is a call to reflect His love to the world. It's a call to be His hands and feet, to demonstrate His love in tangible, real ways, and to show others what the love of God looks like. This love is not always easy, and it often requires sacrifice. But it's the kind of love that changes lives. When we love others as Jesus commands, we are participating in His work of redemption and restoration in the world. We are bringing light into darkness, hope into despair, and healing into brokenness. This is the kind of love that has the power to transform not only individual lives, but entire communities and even the world.

As you continue through "Answer the Call – 31 Days of Bold Biblical Action", let this command to love your neighbor as yourself be a challenge and an invitation to live out the love of Jesus in every area of your life. It's a call to love deeply, to love sacrificially, and to love without limits. It's a call to see others through the eyes of Christ, to extend grace and compassion even when it's hard, and to be the hands and feet of Jesus in a world that desperately needs His love. Let this call to love your neighbor as yourself transform the way you interact with those around you—whether they are family, friends, or strangers. Let it move you to action, to step into the lives of others with a heart full of love, and to be a living testimony of the love of Christ. This is the kind of love that reflects the heart of God, and this is the kind of love that can change the world.

Chapter 6 – Rejoice

In the sixth call to action from "Answer the Call – 31 Days of Bold Biblical Action", we are commanded to "Rejoice evermore" (1 Thessalonians 5:16). These two simple words hold profound meaning, inviting us into a life of constant, unwavering joy—joy that transcends our circumstances, emotions, and experiences. At first glance, this command might seem impossible, especially in a world filled with pain, suffering, disappointment, and hardship. How can we possibly rejoice at all times? How can we maintain a spirit of joy when life throws so many challenges our way? The answer lies not in our circumstances but in the unchanging, unfailing nature of God Himself. To "rejoice evermore" means to anchor our joy in who God is, not in the fleeting and unpredictable events of life. It's about finding our deepest source of happiness, peace, and contentment in the knowledge that God is good, that He loves us, and that His promises are true no matter what we face. This joy isn't dependent on whether things are going well—it's rooted in the assurance that God is with us, working for our good, and leading us toward an eternal future with Him. Rejoicing evermore is an act of faith, an expression of trust, and a declaration of hope that stands firm even in the storm.

To rejoice evermore is to live with a mindset of gratitude. It's about recognizing that, no matter what happens, there is always something to be thankful for because God's blessings are all around us. Even in the hardest times, we can rejoice because we know that God's presence is with us, that His grace is sustaining us, and that His mercies are new every morning. Rejoicing evermore is a way of seeing the world through the lens of God's goodness, choosing to focus on what He has done, what He is doing, and what He will do. It doesn't mean we ignore or deny the reality of pain, suffering, or disappointment—it means that we choose to find joy even in the midst of those challenges by trusting in God's promises. It's about saying, "Even though life is hard right now, I will still rejoice because I know God is good and faithful." This kind of joy is a powerful witness to the world, showing others that our hope is not found in the temporary things of this world, but in the eternal, unshakable foundation of God's love.

The command to rejoice evermore also reminds us that joy is not based on our circumstances, but on our relationship with God. Happiness is often tied to external events—good news, success, comfort, or things going the way we planned. But joy, the kind of joy we are called to have as believers, goes much deeper. It is rooted in the fact that we are loved by God, saved by His grace, and promised an eternal future with Him. This kind of joy cannot be shaken by the ups and downs of life because it is not dependent on those things. It is grounded in the truth of who God is and what He has done for us. When we rejoice evermore, we are choosing to focus on the bigger picture—on God's sovereignty, His goodness, and His faithfulness—rather than getting bogged down by the temporary trials and frustrations of this life. It's about keeping our eyes on Jesus, the source of our joy, and trusting that no matter what we go through, He is with us, He is for us, and He is working all things for our good.

Rejoicing evermore is also a choice we make each day. It's not something that just happens when we feel happy or when life is going smoothly. It's an intentional decision to praise God, to find joy in Him, and to focus on the blessings He has given us, even when it feels difficult. There will be days when rejoicing seems like the last thing we want to do—when we are tired, discouraged, or overwhelmed by the weight of our circumstances. But it is in those moments that rejoicing becomes an act of faith, a way of declaring that we trust God even when we don't understand what is happening. Rejoicing evermore means praising God in the storm, singing His praises even when our hearts are heavy, and finding joy in His presence when everything else feels uncertain. It's about refusing to let the difficulties of life steal the joy that God has given us and choosing, instead, to dwell on the truth of His promises.

This command to rejoice evermore is not a denial of the reality of pain or hardship. God knows that we live in a broken world where suffering is real, where we experience loss, disappointment, and heartache. Jesus Himself was "a man of sorrows" (Isaiah 53:3), and He wept at the tomb of His friend Lazarus (John 11:35). The Bible is full of examples of godly men and women who faced deep grief, hardship, and suffering. But in the midst of their pain, they found a way to rejoice—not because of their circumstances, but because of their faith in God. Paul, who wrote the command to "rejoice evermore," knew suffering all too well. He was beaten, imprisoned, shipwrecked, and faced constant persecution for his faith. Yet he could still write about joy because he knew that his joy was not dependent on his circumstances—it was anchored in Christ. Paul's life shows us that it is possible to experience deep joy even in the midst of great suffering when our joy is rooted in the unchanging love of God.

Rejoicing evermore also means living with an eternal perspective. When we focus solely on the here and now, it's easy to become discouraged by the challenges and hardships we face. But when we lift our eyes to eternity, we are reminded that this life is not all there is. We are reminded that, no matter what we go through in this life, we have the promise of eternal life with God—a life where there will be no more pain, no more suffering, and no more tears. This eternal hope gives us the strength to rejoice even in the midst of trials because we know that our present suffering is temporary, but our future joy is eternal. Rejoicing evermore means keeping our eyes fixed on the hope of heaven, where we will be in the presence of God forever, fully experiencing the joy that He has promised us. To rejoice evermore is also to live in the fullness of the Holy Spirit. Joy is a fruit of the Spirit (Galatians 5:22), and it is the Spirit who empowers us to live lives of joy, even in difficult circumstances. When we are filled with the Spirit, we experience a joy that goes beyond our understanding, a joy that is not based on what is happening around us but on the presence of God within us. The Holy Spirit gives us the strength to rejoice when we feel weak, the comfort to rejoice when we are hurting, and the peace to rejoice when we are anxious. As we walk in step with the Spirit, we find that joy becomes a natural outflow of our relationship with God, a constant source of strength and hope in every season of life.

Rejoicing evermore is also a powerful way to combat worry, fear, and anxiety. When we choose to rejoice, we are choosing to focus on the goodness of God rather than on the problems we are facing. We are choosing to praise Him for who He is and for what He has done, rather than letting our minds be consumed by fear or doubt. Rejoicing lifts our eyes from our circumstances and reminds us of God's power, His faithfulness, and His love. It shifts our focus from what is going wrong to what is going right—from what we lack to the abundance of God's grace in our lives. When we rejoice, we are making a declaration that God is bigger than our problems, that His promises are greater than our fears, and that His presence is enough to sustain us through anything.

Rejoicing evermore is also a way to strengthen our witness to the world. In a world that is often filled with negativity, fear, and hopelessness, a life of joy stands out as a powerful testimony to the goodness of God. When we choose to rejoice in the midst of hardship, when we choose to live with a spirit of gratitude even in difficult times, we show the world that our hope is not in the things of this world but in the God who holds all things in His hands. Our joy becomes a light that draws others to Christ, a reflection of His love and grace. People are drawn to joy because it is rare and precious in a world that often feels dark and heavy. When we live with the joy of the Lord, we become a beacon of hope to those around us, showing them that true, lasting joy is found in a relationship with Jesus.

As you continue through "Answer the Call – 31 Days of Bold Biblical Action", let this command to rejoice evermore be a call to live a life of constant joy, anchored in the unchanging love of God. Let it be a reminder that your joy is not dependent on your circumstances but on your relationship with Christ. Choose to rejoice in every season, in every moment, knowing that God is with you, that His promises are true, and that His love is enough. Let this call to rejoice be an invitation to live in the fullness of the Holy Spirit, to find joy in God's presence, and to trust that He is working all things for your good. Rejoice evermore, knowing that your joy is a powerful testimony to the world of God's goodness, grace, and love. Rejoice evermore, and experience the peace, hope, and strength that come from living a life rooted in the joy of the Lord.

Chapter 7 – Give

In the seventh call to action from "Answer the Call – 31 Days of Bold Biblical Action", we are invited to reflect on the powerful words of Jesus: "Give, and it shall be given unto you; good measure, pressed down, and shaken together, and running over, shall men give into your bosom. For with the same measure that ye mete withal it shall be measured to you again." (Luke 6:38). These words carry a promise that reaches deep into the heart of what it means to live a life of generosity and selflessness, a life that reflects the very nature of God. To give is more than just offering money or material things—it is a posture of the heart, an act of love, and an expression of faith that transforms both the giver and the recipient. When Jesus calls us to give, He is calling us to live with open hands, ready to share not just our resources, but our time, our talents, our love, and our compassion. Giving is an act of trust, an acknowledgment that everything we have comes from God, and that He will provide for our needs even as we give to others. It is a way of participating in God's work of blessing the world, a way of being a vessel through which His love flows to others. But Jesus' promise goes even further—when we give, it will be given back to us. This isn't a promise of material wealth or prosperity, but of the overflowing blessings of God's grace, love, and provision in our lives. When we give generously, we open ourselves to receive the richness of God's blessings in ways that go far beyond what we could ever imagine.

To give as Jesus instructs is to step into a life of generosity that reflects the very heart of God. God is the ultimate giver—He gave us life, He gave us His creation, and most importantly, He gave us His Son, Jesus Christ, as a sacrifice for our sins. The very essence of God's love is expressed through giving, and when we give, we are reflecting His image in the world. Giving is not just about fulfilling a need or meeting a requirement; it is about embodying the love of God in tangible ways. It's about living with a spirit of generosity that goes beyond the minimum and seeks to bless others in the same way that God has blessed us. When we give, we are joining in the mission of God's kingdom, spreading His love, His grace, and His provision to those who need it most. Whether we are giving to those in financial need, offering our time to someone who is lonely, or using our gifts and talents to serve others, we are participating in God's work of redemption and restoration in the world.

Jesus' command to give is also a challenge to our natural tendencies toward self-preservation and accumulation. In a world that often tells us to hold on to what we have, to protect our own interests, and to accumulate more, Jesus calls us to do the opposite. He invites us to live with open hands, trusting that God will provide for us as we give to others. This kind of generosity requires faith. It requires us to believe that God is our provider and that we do not need to fear lack or scarcity. It's easy to give when we feel like we have more than enough, but true generosity is often tested when we are called to give out of our own need or uncertainty. Jesus challenges us to trust that when we give, God will take care of us. This doesn't mean that we give in order to get something in return—it means that we give because we know that our security is not found in our possessions, but in God's faithfulness.

Giving is also a way of breaking the hold that materialism and selfishness can have on our hearts. When we live in a mindset of scarcity, we are often tempted to hold tightly to what we have, fearing that there won't be enough for us. But when we give, we are declaring that we trust God to provide. We are breaking free from the lie that we need to accumulate more in order to be secure or happy. Giving opens our hearts to experience the joy that comes from blessing others, the freedom that comes from releasing our grip on material things, and the peace that comes from trusting God to meet our needs. It reminds us that we are stewards of God's blessings, not owners. Everything we have—our money, our time, our talents—has been given to us by God, and we are called to use those blessings to serve others and glorify Him.

To give, as Jesus teaches, is not just a one-time action; it's a way of life. It's about cultivating a heart of generosity that overflows into every area of our lives. It's about being attentive to the needs around us and being willing to respond, even when it's inconvenient or costly. Jesus calls us to give freely, not grudgingly or out of obligation, but out of a heart that has been transformed by His love. True giving is not about the amount we give—it's about the attitude with which we give. Jesus praised the widow who gave two small coins because she gave out of her poverty, with a heart full of trust in God. Her gift, though small in the eyes of the world, was a reflection of her deep faith and love for God. In the same way, our giving should be motivated by love and faith, not by a desire for recognition or reward.

When we give, we are also building relationships and community. Giving connects us to others in meaningful ways, whether we are supporting someone in need, encouraging a friend, or contributing to a cause that we believe in. It reminds us that we are not isolated individuals, but part of a larger body—the body of Christ. We are called to bear one another's burdens, to rejoice with those who rejoice, and to weep with those who weep. Giving allows us to live out that calling in practical ways. It's a way of showing others that we care, that they are not alone, and that they are loved by God. Whether it's through financial support, acts of service, or simply offering our presence, giving strengthens the bonds of community and reflects the love of Christ to the world.

Jesus' promise that "it shall be given unto you" reminds us that God's economy is not like the world's. In God's kingdom, generosity is always met with more generosity. When we give, we open ourselves to receive—not necessarily in the form of material wealth, but in the form of spiritual blessings, joy, peace, and a deeper relationship with God. God's blessings are often unexpected and come in ways we didn't anticipate. When we give out of love and obedience, God pours out His grace on us in ways that fill our hearts and lives with more than we could ever imagine. This is the mystery of giving: the more we give, the more we receive—not because we are seeking a reward, but because God delights in blessing those who trust Him and live generously.

To give, as Jesus calls us to, is to participate in the flow of God's grace. We are blessed to be a blessing. When we give, we are extending God's love to others, and in return, we experience the joy of being used by Him to make a difference in the world. There is a deep, abiding joy that comes from knowing that we are part of something bigger than ourselves—that through our giving, we are contributing to the work of God's kingdom on earth. This joy is not dependent on how much we have or how much we give; it comes from knowing that we are living in obedience to God's call and that our giving is an act of worship. When we give with a heart full of love and faith, we are participating in God's redemptive work, and that is a source of true and lasting joy.

Jesus' call to give is also a reminder that we are part of a much larger story. Our giving is not just about meeting immediate needs—it's about participating in the eternal purposes of God. When we give, we are investing in God's kingdom, contributing to the work of spreading the gospel, and helping to bring about His plans for the world. Our giving, no matter how small or insignificant it may seem, has eternal value. It's a way of storing up treasures in heaven, where moth and rust do not destroy, and thieves do not break in and steal (Matthew 6:20). Giving is a way of aligning our hearts with God's heart, of prioritizing His kingdom over our own comfort or security, and of trusting that He will use our gifts to accomplish His purposes.

As you continue through "Answer the Call – 31 Days of Bold Biblical Action", let this call to give be an invitation to live a life of generosity, trust, and faith. Let it be a reminder that everything you have is a gift from God and that He is calling you to use those gifts to bless others. Give freely, give joyfully, and give with the confidence that God will provide for your needs. Trust that as you give, God will pour out His blessings on you—blessings of peace, joy, and deeper faith. Let this call to give transform the way you see your resources, your time, and your talents. Let it inspire you to live with open hands, ready to share God's love with a world in need. And as you give, experience the joy and freedom that come from living a life of generosity, knowing that you are participating in the work of God's kingdom and reflecting His heart to those around you.

Chapter 8 – Believe

In the eighth call to action from "Answer the Call – 31 Days of Bold Biblical Action", we encounter one of the most fundamental and powerful commands in all of Scripture: "Believe on the Lord Jesus Christ, and thou shalt be saved" (Acts 16:31). These words capture the very heart of the Christian faith and the message of the gospel. To believe in Jesus is not merely to acknowledge His existence or agree with the idea that He lived in history; it is a deep, personal act of trust that changes everything about who we are, how we live, and where we place our hope. Believing in Jesus is the moment when we turn from our old life and place our faith entirely in Him, trusting that He is who He says He is—our Savior, our Redeemer, and the Son of God who came to rescue us from sin and death. This belief is not just intellectual assent; it is a decision that transforms our hearts, our minds, and our entire lives. It's the difference between living in darkness and being brought into the light, between spiritual death and eternal life. When we believe in Jesus, we are saved—not just from sin, but from the emptiness and brokenness that come from trying to live apart from God.

Belief in Jesus is the foundation upon which everything else in the Christian life is built. It is the starting point of our relationship with God, the moment when we are made new and brought into His family. But this belief is more than just a one-time decision; it is a lifelong commitment to trust and follow Jesus in every area of our lives. When we believe in Jesus, we are not just agreeing with a set of doctrines or subscribing to a religious system—we are surrendering our lives to Him. We are acknowledging that we cannot save ourselves, that we need a Savior, and that Jesus is the only one who can rescue us. This kind of belief requires humility, because it means admitting that we are broken, sinful, and in need of grace. But it also brings incredible freedom, because it means that we no longer have to carry the burden of trying to earn our way to God. Instead, we can rest in the finished work of Jesus on the cross, knowing that our salvation is secure because of His sacrifice.

Believing in Jesus is about placing our full trust in Him, not just for our salvation, but for every part of our lives. It means trusting that He is who He says He is—the Son of God who came to earth, lived a perfect life, died on the cross for our sins, and rose again, conquering death. It means believing that His death was enough to pay the penalty for our sins, that His resurrection is the proof of His victory, and that through Him, we are forgiven, redeemed, and given eternal life. But this belief is not just about what Jesus did in the past—it's also about what He is doing in our lives right now. To believe in Jesus is to trust Him with our present and our future, to rely on Him for guidance, strength, and hope in every situation. It's about recognizing that He is Lord, not just of the world, but of our own personal lives, and choosing to follow Him wherever He leads.

When we believe in Jesus, something incredible happens: we are saved. This is not just a theological concept or a future promise—it is a reality that we experience here and now. Salvation means that we are rescued from the power of sin, that we are forgiven for every wrong we have ever done, and that we are given new life in Christ. It means that our past no longer defines us, that our sins are washed away, and that we are free to live as new creations. Salvation is the greatest gift we could ever receive, and it is offered to us freely, not because of anything we have done, but because of God's incredible love and grace. When we believe in Jesus, we are not just saved from something—we are saved for something. We are saved to live in relationship with God, to experience His love, and to live out His purpose for our lives. We are saved to be part of His kingdom, to join in His mission of bringing hope, healing, and redemption to the world.

But what does it really mean to believe in Jesus? It means more than just saying the words—it means trusting Him with our whole hearts. It means turning away from the things we used to trust in—whether that's our own abilities, our accomplishments, or anything else we relied on for meaning and security—and placing all of our trust in Jesus alone. It means accepting His invitation to follow Him, to let Him lead our lives, and to surrender our will to His. This kind of belief is not passive; it is active and dynamic. It's a belief that changes the way we live, because when we truly believe in Jesus, we are transformed from the inside out. We begin to see the world differently, through the lens of His love and grace. We start to live with a new purpose, because we are no longer living for ourselves—we are living for Him.

Believing in Jesus also means trusting Him in the midst of life's challenges. It's easy to believe when things are going well, but true belief is tested in the difficult moments—when we face trials, suffering, or uncertainty. In those times, believing in Jesus means holding on to the truth that He is with us, that He is for us, and that He is working all things for our good, even when we can't see it. It means trusting that He is bigger than our problems, that He has overcome the world, and that nothing can separate us from His love. This kind of belief gives us strength, peace, and hope, even in the darkest moments, because we know that Jesus is our rock, our refuge, and our Savior.

The call to believe in Jesus is a call to faith, but it is also a call to action. When we believe in Jesus, we are not just saved for ourselves—we are called to share that good news with others. Belief in Jesus compels us to live out our faith in the way we love, serve, and care for others. It moves us to be His hands and feet in the world, to share the hope we have found in Him with those who are lost, hurting, and searching for meaning. When we truly believe in Jesus, we cannot keep that joy and hope to ourselves—we are called to go out into the world and make disciples, to tell others about the incredible love of God and the salvation that is available through Christ.

But belief is not always easy. There are times when doubts creep in, when the challenges of life make us question what we believe. In those moments, it's important to remember that belief is not about having all the answers—it's about trusting the One who does. Faith is not the absence of doubt; it's choosing to trust Jesus even when we don't have everything figured out. It's holding on to the promises of God, even when we can't see the outcome. Jesus never promised that life would be easy, but He did promise that He would be with us always, and that He would never leave us or forsake us. Believing in Jesus means trusting Him through the uncertainties, knowing that He is faithful and that His love never fails.

To believe in Jesus is also to experience the incredible love of God in a personal way. When we place our faith in Him, we are not just saved from our sins—we are brought into a relationship with the God who created us, loves us, and knows us better than anyone else. This relationship is the most important part of our lives, because it is through this relationship that we experience true peace, joy, and fulfillment. Believing in Jesus means knowing that we are loved unconditionally, that we are valued beyond measure, and that our identity is found in Him. This love is not something we have to earn—it is a gift that is freely given to us by God's grace. When we believe in Jesus, we are adopted into God's family, and we can rest in the assurance that we are His children, loved and cherished by Him for all eternity.

As you continue through "Answer the Call – 31 Days of Bold Biblical Action", let this call to believe in Jesus be an invitation to place your trust fully in Him. If you have never made the decision to believe in Jesus, know that this is the most important decision you will ever make. Jesus is inviting you to come to Him, to trust Him with your life, and to receive the gift of salvation that He offers. If you have already placed your faith in Jesus, let this call be a reminder to continue trusting Him in every area of your life. Let it be an encouragement to deepen your relationship with Him, to follow Him more closely, and to live out your faith with boldness and courage. Believing in Jesus is not just a one-time event—it is a lifelong journey of trusting, following, and growing in Him.

Believe in Jesus, and you will be saved. Believe in Jesus, and you will experience the love, grace, and forgiveness of God. Believe in Jesus, and you will find hope, peace, and purpose for your life. This is the promise of the gospel, the good news that changes everything. When we believe in Jesus, we are made new, we are given eternal life, and we are invited into a relationship with the God who loves us more than we could ever imagine. Believe on the Lord Jesus Christ, and watch as He transforms your heart, your life, and your eternity.

Chapter 9 – Forgive

In the ninth call to action from "Answer the Call – 31 Days of Bold Biblical Action", we are presented with one of the most difficult and yet freeing commands in Scripture: "Judge not, and ye shall not be judged: condemn not, and ye shall not be condemned: forgive, and ye shall be forgiven" (Luke 6:37). Forgiveness is one of the most powerful and life-altering choices we can make, yet it is often one of the hardest. To forgive someone who has hurt us—whether it's a friend who betrayed us, a family member who caused us pain, or even a stranger who wronged us—goes against our natural instincts. Our human nature wants to hold on to anger, bitterness, and resentment. We want to protect ourselves from being hurt again, and we often feel that if we forgive, we are letting the other person off the hook. But Jesus' command to forgive goes far deeper than simply letting go of a grudge. It's a call to release the debt that we believe others owe us, to let go of the poison of bitterness, and to step into the freedom that only forgiveness can bring. Forgiveness is not about excusing the wrong or pretending it didn't happen—it's about choosing to release the hold that the offense has on us and trusting God to bring healing and justice in His perfect way and timing.

When Jesus tells us to forgive, He is asking us to follow His example. No one understands the cost of forgiveness better than Jesus. He was betrayed, beaten, mocked, and crucified—yet as He hung on the cross, He prayed, "Father, forgive them, for they know not what they do" (Luke 23:34). Jesus forgave those who nailed Him to the cross, and He forgave each of us for our sins. He bore the weight of our wrongs so that we could be forgiven and reconciled to God. This is the heart of the gospel: we are forgiven not because of anything we have done to deserve it, but because of God's incredible love and grace. When we realize how much we have been forgiven, it changes everything. It changes the way we see ourselves, and it changes the way we see others. When we truly grasp the depth of God's forgiveness toward us, we are compelled to extend that same forgiveness to others.

Forgiveness is not just something we do for the other person—it's something we do for ourselves. When we hold on to anger, bitterness, and resentment, it becomes like a heavy chain around our hearts, weighing us down and preventing us from experiencing the peace and freedom that God wants for us. Unforgiveness can consume us, stealing our joy and filling our minds with thoughts of revenge or resentment. It can even affect our physical health, as stress and bitterness take a toll on our bodies. But when we choose to forgive, we are releasing ourselves from the prison of bitterness. We are choosing to lay down the burden of unforgiveness and trust God to heal our hearts. Forgiveness is not easy—it can be painful, and it often requires us to confront the hurt and the injustice that was done to us. But it is also one of the most freeing choices we can make. When we forgive, we are choosing to let go of the past and move forward into the future that God has for us.

Jesus' command to forgive is not conditional—it doesn't depend on whether the other person deserves it, whether they have apologized, or whether they have changed. Forgiveness is a choice that we make regardless of the other person's actions. This can be incredibly difficult because, in our human sense of justice, we want to wait for the other person to make things right before we forgive. But Jesus calls us to a higher standard. He calls us to forgive just as He has forgiven us—freely, unconditionally, and completely. This doesn't mean that we are excusing the wrong or minimizing the hurt that was caused. It simply means that we are choosing to release the other person from the debt we believe they owe us, and we are trusting God to bring justice in His way and His time.

Forgiveness is an act of faith. It's about trusting that God is the ultimate judge and that He will bring justice in the end. It's about releasing our need for revenge or retribution and trusting that God sees the hurt, the injustice, and the pain, and that He will make things right. When we forgive, we are surrendering our desire to control the situation and placing it in God's hands. This doesn't mean that we are ignoring the wrong or that we have to continue to put ourselves in a position to be hurt again. Forgiveness doesn't always mean reconciliation, especially in cases where there is ongoing harm or danger. But it does mean that we are choosing to let go of the bitterness and entrusting the situation to God, knowing that He is the ultimate source of justice and healing.

One of the most important aspects of forgiveness is the healing it brings to our own hearts. When we choose to forgive, we are allowing God to heal the wounds that unforgiveness has created. Forgiveness doesn't happen overnight—it's often a process that takes time and requires us to continually surrender the hurt to God. But as we choose to forgive, day by day, we experience the healing power of God's love and grace. We begin to feel the weight of bitterness lift from our hearts, and we find freedom in knowing that we are no longer defined by the hurt that was done to us. Forgiveness allows us to move forward, to experience peace, and to live in the fullness of God's grace.

Jesus' promise that "ye shall be forgiven" reminds us that forgiveness is not just something we are called to give—it's something we have received. We have all sinned and fallen short of the glory of God (Romans 3:23), and yet God, in His great mercy, has forgiven us. He has wiped our slate clean, removed our sins as far as the east is from the west (Psalm 103:12), and given us a new identity as His beloved children. When we forgive others, we are reflecting the forgiveness that we have received from God. We are showing the world the power of God's grace and the transformative love of Christ. Forgiveness is not just about the past—it's about the future. It's about creating space for healing, reconciliation, and new beginnings. When we forgive, we are opening the door to restoration and allowing God to work in ways that we could never imagine.

Forgiveness is also a powerful witness to the world. In a world that often holds on to grudges, seeks revenge, and harbors bitterness, the act of forgiveness stands out as a radical expression of love and grace. When we choose to forgive, we are reflecting the heart of Jesus to a watching world. We are showing that love is stronger than hate, that grace is more powerful than vengeance, and that forgiveness can bring healing and reconciliation where there was once division and pain. Forgiveness is not weakness—it is strength. It takes courage to forgive, to let go of the desire for revenge, and to choose love instead of bitterness. But in doing so, we are demonstrating the power of the gospel and the love of Christ in a way that speaks louder than words.

To forgive is to live in the freedom that Christ has won for us. When we hold on to unforgiveness, we are allowing the past to keep us in chains. But when we forgive, we are stepping into the freedom that Jesus offers. We are choosing to live in the light of His grace, knowing that we are forgiven, loved, and set free. Forgiveness is not a one-time act—it's a way of life. It's a daily decision to release bitterness, to extend grace, and to trust God with our hurts. It's about living with open hands, ready to forgive, because we know that we have been forgiven much.

As you continue through "Answer the Call – 31 Days of Bold Biblical Action", let this call to forgive be an invitation to experience the freedom and healing that come from living a life of grace. If there is someone in your life that you need to forgive, ask God for the strength and courage to take that step. It may not be easy, and it may take time, but as you choose to forgive, you will experience the peace and joy that come from releasing the burden of unforgiveness. Let this call to forgive be a reminder that you are forgiven by God, and that His grace is sufficient for every hurt, every pain, and every wound. Forgive, and you shall be forgiven. This is the promise of the gospel—when we forgive, we are stepping into the fullness of God's love, grace, and healing.

Forgive, and watch as God brings healing to your heart, restoration to your relationships, and freedom to your soul. Forgive, and experience the joy of living in the grace and love of Jesus.

Chapter 10 – Follow

In the tenth call to action from "Answer the Call – 31 Days of Bold Biblical Action", we encounter one of the most life-altering commands Jesus ever gave: "And he saith unto them, Follow me, and I will make you fishers of men." (Matthew 4:19). These simple words from Jesus are more than just an invitation—they are a call to leave behind the familiar, the comfortable, and the ordinary in exchange for something far greater: a life of purpose, meaning, and eternal impact. When Jesus called His first disciples, they were ordinary fishermen going about their daily routines. But when He said, "Follow me," everything changed. They immediately left their nets, their boats, and their livelihoods behind to follow Jesus. This moment wasn't just a decision to walk with Jesus physically—it was a decision to entrust their entire lives to Him, to submit to His authority, and to become part of something much bigger than themselves. Jesus wasn't just inviting them to follow Him for a day or a week—He was calling them to a lifelong journey of transformation and mission. And that same invitation is extended to each of us today. "Follow me" is not a suggestion or a casual request—it is a command that requires a response, a decision that will shape the course of our lives. It is a call to surrender, to trust, and to walk in the footsteps of the Savior who gave everything for us.

To follow Jesus is to embark on a journey of radical faith and obedience. It's not about following Him from a distance or simply admiring His teachings—it's about walking closely with Him, allowing Him to lead every aspect of our lives. When we follow Jesus, we are saying, "Lord, I trust You with my whole heart. I am willing to go wherever You lead, to do whatever You ask, and to leave behind anything that holds me back from fully surrendering to You." This kind of following requires sacrifice, but it also brings freedom. Following Jesus means letting go of our old ways, our old priorities, and our old identities. It means leaving behind the things that once defined us—whether it's our career, our ambitions, our habits, or our fears—and finding our true identity in Christ. When we follow Jesus, we are no longer defined by what the world says about us or by our past mistakes. We are defined by the love, grace, and purpose that Jesus gives us.

But following Jesus is not just about what we leave behind—it's about what we are stepping into. When Jesus called His disciples to follow Him, He promised to make them "fishers of men." In other words, He was inviting them to join Him in His mission of bringing hope, salvation, and the good news of the gospel to the world. Following Jesus means that we are not just saved for ourselves—we are saved for a purpose. We are called to be part of God's redemptive plan for humanity, to be His hands and feet in the world, and to share the love of Christ with those who are lost, hurting, and in need of a Savior. To be a "fisher of men" means that we are actively engaged in sharing the gospel, reaching out to others with the message of hope and salvation, and inviting them to follow Jesus as well. This is not a task reserved for pastors or missionaries—this is the calling of every believer. When we follow Jesus, we are called to make disciples, to spread the light of Christ, and to be a witness to the transforming power of His love.

Following Jesus also means walking in step with His example. Throughout His ministry, Jesus modeled what it means to love selflessly, serve humbly, and sacrifice for the sake of others. When He washed the feet of His disciples, He showed them that true leadership is about servanthood, not power. When He healed the sick and fed the hungry, He demonstrated His compassion and care for the least and the lost. And when He went to the cross, He gave the ultimate example of sacrificial love, laying down His life so that we might live. To follow Jesus is to follow in His footsteps, to live as He lived, and to love as He loved. It's about putting others before ourselves, seeking justice for the oppressed, showing mercy to the broken, and offering forgiveness to those who have wronged us. It's about living a life that reflects the heart of God and points others to the hope and healing that can only be found in Jesus.

But following Jesus is not always easy. There will be times when the road is difficult, when we face opposition, trials, or uncertainty. There will be moments when we are tempted to turn back, to return to the safety and comfort of our old lives. But Jesus never promised that following Him would be easy—He promised that it would be worth it. He said, "If anyone would come after me, let him deny himself and take up his cross daily and follow me" (Luke 9:23). Following Jesus requires us to lay down our own desires, our own plans, and our own agendas, and to trust Him completely. It means being willing to endure hardship, persecution, or sacrifice for the sake of the gospel. But in the midst of the challenges, we are never alone. Jesus walks with us every step of the way, giving us the strength, courage, and grace we need to continue following Him, even when the path is hard.

One of the most beautiful aspects of following Jesus is the transformation that takes place in our lives. As we follow Him, we are changed from the inside out. We begin to think differently, love differently, and live differently. The more time we spend with Jesus, the more we become like Him. Our hearts are softened, our priorities are shifted, and our desires are aligned with His will. Following Jesus doesn't just change our external behavior—it changes our hearts. It transforms us into people who reflect the character of Christ, who love God with all our hearts, and who love our neighbors as ourselves. This transformation is not something we can achieve on our own—it is the work of the Holy Spirit in our lives. As we follow Jesus, He is continually shaping us, molding us, and refining us into the people He created us to be.

Following Jesus also brings us into community with other believers. When Jesus called His disciples, He didn't call them to follow Him alone—He called them to follow Him together. As followers of Jesus, we are part of a larger family, the body of Christ. We are called to walk alongside one another, to encourage one another, to pray for one another, and to hold each other accountable. Following Jesus is not a solo journey—it's a journey we take together, supporting and strengthening one another along the way. This sense of community is one of the greatest gifts of following Jesus. It reminds us that we are not alone, that we are part of something bigger than ourselves, and that we have a family of believers who are walking with us, cheering us on, and helping us grow in our faith.

When Jesus says, "Follow me," He is not just calling us to a new way of life—He is calling us into a relationship with Him. Following Jesus is not about following a set of rules or living up to a list of expectations—it's about knowing Him personally, walking with Him daily, and experiencing the love and grace that only He can give. Jesus wants more than just our obedience—He wants our hearts. He wants us to know Him, to trust Him, and to love Him with all that we are. Following Jesus means spending time in His presence, listening to His voice, and allowing Him to lead us and guide us. It's about developing a deep, intimate relationship with the One who knows us better than we know ourselves and who loves us more than we can imagine.

As you continue through "Answer the Call – 31 Days of Bold Biblical Action", let this call to follow Jesus be an invitation to step into the life He has for you. If you have never made the decision to follow Jesus, know that He is inviting you today to leave behind your old life and follow Him into a life of purpose, freedom, and joy. He is calling you to trust Him with your heart, your future, and your eternity. If you have already made the decision to follow Jesus, let this call be a reminder to follow Him more closely, to surrender more fully, and to trust Him more deeply. Following Jesus is not just a one-time decision—it's a daily choice to walk with Him, to listen to Him, and to live for Him. It's a journey that will take us to places we never expected, but it's a journey that will lead us to life—abundant, eternal life in Christ.

"Follow me, and I will make you fishers of men." These words of Jesus are both a promise and a calling. As we follow Him, He promises to transform us, to equip us, and to use us for His purposes. He invites us to be part of His mission to reach the lost, to heal the broken, and to bring the hope of the gospel to a world in need. Following Jesus is not just about what He can do for us—it's about what He wants to do through us. He has a purpose for each of our lives, and when we follow Him, we step into that purpose. We become part of His kingdom work, sharing His love, His truth, and His grace with others.

Follow Jesus, and watch as He transforms your heart, your life, and your future. Follow Jesus, and experience the joy, peace, and purpose that only He can give. Follow Jesus, and be part of His mission to bring hope and salvation to the world. This is the greatest calling, the greatest adventure, and the greatest privilege we could ever have. Follow Jesus, and never look back.

Chapter 11 – Trust

In the eleventh call to action from "Answer the Call – 31 Days of Bold Biblical Action", we are commanded to " Trust in the LORD with all thine heart; and lean not unto thine own understanding." (Proverbs 3:5). This verse is one of the most comforting and yet challenging instructions in Scripture because it invites us to place our full, undivided trust in God, not just with part of our hearts, but with all of it. To trust in the Lord with all our hearts means that we are called to surrender every aspect of our lives—our hopes, our fears, our future, our present circumstances, and even our disappointments—into His hands, fully confident that He is good, faithful, and sovereign over everything. It's an invitation to let go of the control we often cling to and instead rely completely on God's wisdom, His timing, and His perfect plan for our lives. This trust is not a passive, wishful thinking kind of trust—it's an active, deliberate choice to believe that God knows best, that His ways are higher than our ways, and that His thoughts are higher than our thoughts (Isaiah 55:9). It's the kind of trust that anchors our hearts in the midst of life's storms, that holds us steady when everything around us is shaking, and that fills us with peace even when the future seems uncertain.

Trusting in the Lord with all our hearts means that we are choosing to believe in God's goodness, even when our circumstances don't make sense. It's easy to trust God when everything is going well, when our prayers are being answered the way we want, and when life feels manageable. But the real test of trust comes when life takes unexpected turns—when we face challenges, heartache, loss, or confusion. In those moments, trusting in the Lord means choosing to believe that He is still in control, that He is still good, and that He is still working all things together for our good (Romans 8:28), even when we can't see it. This kind of trust requires faith, because it asks us to rely not on what we see or feel, but on the character and promises of God. Trusting in the

Lord with all our hearts means that we choose to trust Him not just with the good parts of our lives, but also with the messy, broken, and uncertain parts. It's about surrendering our desire to understand everything and instead resting in the knowledge that God understands everything, and that He is working in ways we may not yet perceive.

To trust in the Lord with all our hearts is to lean not on our own understanding. Proverbs 3:5 reminds us that our own understanding is limited, flawed, and often influenced by fear, doubt, and worldly thinking. Our human tendency is to rely on our own logic, our own plans, and our own strength to navigate life's challenges. We want to have everything figured out, to know what's going to happen next, and to control the outcome of our circumstances. But God calls us to a different way of living—He calls us to lean not on our own understanding, but to trust in His wisdom and guidance. This doesn't mean that we ignore wisdom, common sense, or planning, but it does mean that we submit all of our understanding to God's greater wisdom. It's about recognizing that God sees the whole picture, while we only see a small part. He knows what's best for us, even when we don't. Trusting in the Lord with all our hearts means that we stop trying to figure everything out on our own and instead seek His direction in every aspect of our lives.

Trusting in the Lord with all our hearts also means trusting His timing. One of the hardest things about trust is waiting—waiting for God to answer our prayers, waiting for Him to move in a situation, or waiting for Him to bring clarity and direction. It's in the waiting that our trust is often tested the most, because we want things to happen on our schedule. But God's timing is perfect, and when we trust Him with all our hearts, we are acknowledging that His timing is better than ours. Trusting in the Lord means waiting patiently for Him to act, knowing that He is never late, and that His plans are always good. It's about surrendering our desire for immediate answers and instead trusting that God is working behind the scenes, preparing us for what's ahead, and orchestrating everything according to His perfect will. Trusting God's timing can be difficult, especially when we don't see the answers we're hoping for, but it's in these moments that our trust is strengthened, as we learn to rely on God's faithfulness and His promises.

Another aspect of trusting in the Lord with all our hearts is trusting Him with our fears and anxieties. Life is full of uncertainties, and it's natural to feel anxious or fearful about the future. But God calls us to cast all our cares on Him because He cares for us (1 Peter 5:7). When we trust in the Lord, we are choosing to let go of our fears and place them in His hands, believing that He is bigger than anything we could ever face. Trusting God doesn't mean that we will never experience fear or anxiety, but it does mean that we don't have to be controlled by them. We can bring our fears to God, lay them at His feet, and trust that He will give us the peace that surpasses all understanding (Philippians 4:6-7). Trusting in the Lord with all our hearts means that we refuse to let worry and fear dictate our decisions or steal our joy. Instead, we choose to trust that God is in control, that He is with us, and that He will provide everything we need.

Trusting in the Lord with all our hearts also means trusting Him with our future. We live in a world that often tells us to take control of our own destinies, to plan every detail of our lives, and to rely on our own strength to succeed. But as followers of Jesus, we are called to a different way of living—a way that acknowledges that our lives are not our own, and that God is the one who holds our future. When we trust in the Lord with all our hearts, we are surrendering our plans, our dreams, and our ambitions to Him, believing that His plans for us are better than anything we could ever imagine. This doesn't mean that we stop setting goals or making plans, but it does mean that we hold our plans loosely, always ready to surrender them to God's will. It means trusting that even when our plans don't work out the way we hoped, God is still in control, and that He has a purpose and a plan for our lives that is far greater than we could ever dream.

To trust in the Lord with all our hearts is also to trust Him in the midst of pain and suffering. Life is filled with moments of heartache, loss, and disappointment, and in those moments, it can be hard to understand why God would allow us to go through such difficult trials. But trusting in the Lord means believing that even in the darkest moments, God is still with us, that He is still good, and that He is working all things for our good. It's about holding on to the truth that God is our refuge and strength, a very present help in trouble (Psalm 46:1). Trusting in the Lord doesn't mean that we will never experience pain, but it does mean that we can find hope and peace in the midst of it, knowing that God is using our pain to draw us closer to Him and to accomplish His purposes in our lives. Trusting God in the midst of suffering is one of the most difficult things we can do, but it's also one of the most powerful, because it deepens our faith and reminds us that we are never alone.

When we trust in the Lord with all our hearts, we are choosing to live a life of surrender and faith. It's about letting go of our need to control everything and instead placing our lives fully in God's hands. It's about trusting that He is good, that He loves us, and that His plans for us are better than anything we could ever imagine. Trusting in the Lord is not a one-time decision—it's a daily choice to surrender our hearts, our minds, and our lives to Him, believing that He is faithful and that He will never let us down. It's about walking by faith, not by sight (2 Corinthians 5:7), and trusting that even when we don't understand what's happening, God is still in control.

As you continue through "Answer the Call – 31 Days of Bold Biblical Action", let this call to trust in the Lord with all your heart be an invitation to experience the peace and freedom that come from placing your trust fully in God. If there are areas of your life where you have been holding back, trying to rely on your own understanding or strength, now is the time to surrender them to God. Trust Him with your heart, your fears, your future, and your circumstances. Trust Him in the waiting, in the uncertainty, and in the midst of the storm. Trust Him with all that you are, knowing that He is faithful and that He will never let you down.

Trust in the Lord with all your heart, and watch as He leads you, guides you, and provides for you in ways that you could never have imagined. Trust Him with your hopes and dreams, and know that He has a purpose and a plan for your life that is far greater than anything you could ever dream. Trust Him in the moments of joy, and trust Him in the moments of pain, knowing that He is with you every step of the way. Trust Him with all your heart, and experience the peace, joy, and freedom that come from living a life fully surrendered to the God who loves you, knows you, and holds your future in His hands. Trust in the Lord with all your heart, and rest in the assurance that He is faithful, He is good, and He is working all things together for your good.

Chapter 12 – Serve

In the twelfth call to action from "Answer the Call – 31 Days of Bold Biblical Action", we are given a beautiful and life-changing command from Scripture: "Serve the LORD with gladness: come before his presence with singing." (Psalm 100:2). These words remind us that serving God is not just a duty or obligation, but a privilege that fills our lives with joy, purpose, and meaning. To serve the Lord with gladness means that we approach every act of service with a heart full of gratitude, knowing that we have the honor of working alongside the Creator of the universe to accomplish His purposes on earth. It means recognizing that God has given each of us unique gifts, talents, and opportunities to make a difference in the lives of others and to bring glory to His name. This call to serve with gladness is not just about the outward actions we take—whether it's volunteering at church, helping a neighbor, or sharing the gospel—it's about the attitude of our hearts as we serve. God doesn't just want our hands; He wants our hearts. He wants us to serve Him with joy, with a sense of gratitude for all He has done for us, and with a deep love for Him and for others. When we serve with gladness, our service becomes an act of worship, a way to express our love and devotion to God, and a reflection of the joy that comes from knowing Him.

To serve the Lord with gladness is to embrace the reality that every moment of our lives can be an opportunity to serve Him. Whether we are working in our jobs, raising our children, caring for a loved one, or simply interacting with others throughout the day, we can serve the Lord in everything we do. Serving God is not limited to the big, public acts of service; it is found in the small, everyday moments of life where we choose to put others before ourselves, to love without expecting anything in return, and to glorify God in all that we do. Serving the Lord with gladness means that we approach each day with a sense of purpose, knowing that even the most ordinary tasks can be done for His glory.

It's about having an attitude that says, "Lord, how can I serve You today? How can I be Your hands and feet to those around me? How can I reflect Your love in the way I live and serve others?" This kind of heart posture transforms the way we see our lives, our work, and our relationships, because it reminds us that we are part of something much bigger than ourselves—we are part of God's kingdom, and everything we do has eternal significance.

But serving the Lord with gladness is not always easy. There will be times when we feel tired, unappreciated, or overwhelmed by the demands of life. In those moments, it can be tempting to serve out of a sense of obligation or duty, rather than out of gladness. But Psalm 100:2 challenges us to shift our perspective, to remember why we serve and who we are serving. When we remember that we are serving the Lord—the One who loved us enough to send His Son to die for us, the One who forgave our sins and gave us new life—it fills our hearts with joy. Serving the Lord is not a burden; it is a blessing. It's an opportunity to partner with the God of the universe in His work of redemption, restoration, and love. When we focus on the incredible privilege it is to serve the Lord, our hearts are filled with gladness, and we are able to serve with joy, even in the midst of challenges.

Serving the Lord with gladness also means serving others with love and humility. Jesus Himself set the perfect example of what it means to serve. Throughout His life on earth, He demonstrated what true service looks like—not seeking to be served, but to serve others (Mark 10:45). From washing the feet of His disciples to healing the sick, feeding the hungry, and ultimately laying down His life on the cross, Jesus showed us that serving others is at the very heart of what it means to follow Him. When we serve others, we are not just doing good deeds; we are following in the footsteps of our Savior. We are reflecting His love, His compassion, and His humility to a world that desperately needs to see Him. To serve the Lord with gladness is to serve others with the same love, grace, and humility that Jesus showed us. It's about seeing every person as someone created in the image of God, someone who is deeply loved by Him, and someone who deserves to be treated with kindness, respect, and care.

One of the most powerful aspects of serving the Lord with gladness is that it changes us. When we serve with a joyful heart, we experience the incredible truth that it is more blessed to give than to receive (Acts 20:35). Serving others with gladness fills us with a sense of purpose and fulfillment that nothing else can provide. It takes our focus off of ourselves and our own problems and reminds us that we are part of something bigger. It helps us see the needs of others and opens our hearts to compassion. As we serve with gladness, we become more like Jesus, growing in humility, love, and selflessness. Serving others with joy also deepens our relationship with God because it allows us to experience His heart for the world. When we serve, we are entering into God's work, and we begin to see people and situations the way He sees them. This kind of service is transformative—not just for those we serve, but for us as well.

But serving the Lord with gladness is not about seeking recognition or praise. True service is done with a heart that seeks to glorify God, not to elevate ourselves. Jesus warned against serving for the purpose of being seen by others or receiving human applause (Matthew 6:1-4). Instead, He calls us to serve with humility, knowing that our reward comes from God, not from people. When we serve the Lord with gladness, we are not seeking the approval or recognition of others—we are simply serving out of love for God and a desire to honor Him. This kind of service is done in secret, in the quiet moments where no one else is watching, but God sees. It's the kind of service that flows from a heart that has been transformed by His grace, a heart that desires to give back in response to all that God has done for us.

To serve the Lord with gladness also means serving without grumbling or complaining. In Philippians 2:14-15, Paul reminds us to "do all things without grumbling or disputing, that you may be blameless and innocent, children of God without blemish in the midst of a crooked and twisted generation, among whom you shine as lights in the world." Serving with gladness is not about doing the bare minimum or serving with a bad attitude. It's about serving with a heart that is full of gratitude and joy, even when the task is hard or thankless. This kind of service stands out in a world where complaining and negativity are often the norm. When we serve with gladness, we shine as lights in the darkness, reflecting the love and joy of Christ to those around us.

Serving the Lord with gladness is also about trusting Him with the results. Sometimes, we may serve faithfully, but we don't see immediate results or the impact of our efforts. We may wonder if our service is making a difference or if anyone even notices. But serving the Lord with gladness means trusting that God is working, even when we can't see it. It's about believing that every act of service, no matter how small, matters to God and is part of His larger plan. When we serve with gladness, we are trusting that God will take our efforts, multiply them, and use them for His glory. We may not always see the fruit of our service in this life, but we can trust that God sees, and that He is faithful to use our service for His kingdom purposes.

Another important aspect of serving the Lord with gladness is serving with others. We are not called to serve the Lord in isolation, but as part of a community of believers. When we serve alongside others, we encourage one another, strengthen one another, and build each other up in love. Serving with others also reminds us that we are part of the body of Christ, and that each of us has a unique role to play. When we serve together, we reflect the unity and love of Christ to the world. Serving with gladness as part of a community also helps us stay focused on the joy of serving, rather than on the challenges or difficulties we may face. It reminds us that we are not alone in this journey, and that together, we can accomplish far more than we could on our own.

As you continue through "Answer the Call – 31 Days of Bold Biblical Action", let this call to serve the Lord with gladness be an invitation to experience the joy and fulfillment that come from a life of service. If there are areas of your life where you have been holding back from serving, or if you have been serving out of a sense of obligation rather than joy, ask God to fill your heart with gladness and gratitude for the opportunity to serve Him. Ask Him to give you a heart that delights in serving others, a heart that reflects His love and grace. Let this call to serve with gladness remind you that every act of service, no matter how small, is a way to honor God and bring glory to His name. Whether you are serving in your home, your workplace, your church, or your community, know that God is using your service to accomplish His purposes and to bring His kingdom to earth.

Serve the Lord with gladness, and experience the joy and fulfillment that come from being part of His work. Serve with a heart full of love, gratitude, and humility, knowing that you are reflecting the heart of Christ to the world. Serve with gladness, and trust that God is using your service in ways that you may not even see. Serve the Lord with gladness, and be a light in a world that desperately needs to see the love, hope, and joy of Jesus. Serve the Lord with gladness, and watch as He fills your heart with peace, purpose, and joy that can only come from knowing and serving Him.

Chapter 13 – Stand

In the thirteenth call to action from "Answer the Call – 31 Days of Bold Biblical Action", we are confronted with the powerful command to "Stand therefore, having your loins girt about with truth, and having on the breastplate of righteousness" (Ephesians 6:14). This instruction from the Apostle Paul, found in his description of the armor of God, reminds us that as believers, we are called to stand firm in our faith, anchored in the truth of God's Word. To "stand" means to be unmovable, unwavering, and resolute in our convictions, especially in the face of adversity, temptation, or spiritual attack. It means that when the world around us shifts, when challenges arise, and when doubts creep in, we remain rooted in the unchanging truth of who God is, what He has done for us through Jesus Christ, and the promises He has given us. This kind of standing is not passive—it is an active, intentional choice to cling to the truth of God's Word and to stand firm in our faith, no matter what comes our way. We are called to stand in the midst of a spiritual battle, and this standing requires strength, courage, and reliance on the armor that God provides.

The imagery of "girding your loins with truth" paints a vivid picture of preparation and readiness. In ancient times, soldiers would gird their loins—tie up the long, loose parts of their garments—before going into battle, so they could move freely and avoid being tripped up. In the same way, we are called to gird ourselves with truth, to wrap ourselves in the truth of God's Word, so that we can stand strong and not be tripped up by the lies and deceptions of the enemy. Truth is foundational to our ability to stand firm in the face of spiritual attack. Without truth, we are vulnerable to confusion, doubt, and the shifting opinions of the world around us. But when we are grounded in the truth of God's Word, we are able to stand with confidence, knowing that His truth is unchanging, reliable, and powerful. To gird our loins with truth means that we immerse ourselves in Scripture, allowing God's Word to shape our minds, our hearts, and our actions. It means that we are not swayed by the opinions of others or the trends of society, but that we stand firm in the eternal truth of God's promises.

Standing with our loins girt about with truth also means standing in the face of spiritual warfare. Paul's words in Ephesians 6:14 are part of a larger passage that describes the armor of God, which is given to us to withstand the attacks of the enemy. The truth of God's Word is our primary defense against the lies, accusations, and temptations that Satan throws our way. The enemy will try to deceive us, to make us doubt God's love, His goodness, or His plan for our lives. He will try to sow confusion, fear, and discouragement in our hearts. But when we are girded with the truth of God's Word, we are able to stand firm against these attacks, knowing that God's truth is greater than any lie the enemy can throw at us. The truth of Scripture reminds us of who we are in Christ—that we are forgiven, redeemed, and loved by God. It reminds us of God's faithfulness, His power, and His promises to never leave us or forsake us. When we stand on this truth, we are able to resist the enemy and remain steadfast in our faith, no matter what battles we face.

But standing firm in the truth doesn't just protect us from external attacks—it also strengthens us from within. When we live in the truth of God's Word, we are filled with a deep sense of peace, security, and confidence. We know that our identity is not found in the opinions of others or in our accomplishments, but in who God says we are. We know that our hope is not based on the circumstances of this world, but on the eternal promises of God. This kind of confidence allows us to stand firm in the midst of uncertainty, to hold on to hope when things seem hopeless, and to trust God's plan even when we don't fully understand it. When we stand in the truth of God's Word, we are able to weather the storms of life with a sense of peace and assurance, knowing that God is in control and that His truth will always prevail.

Standing with our loins girt about with truth also means standing for what is right and true in a world that often rejects God's standards. As believers, we are called to be a light in the darkness, to stand for justice, righteousness, and truth, even when it is unpopular or difficult. This kind of standing requires courage, because it often means going against the flow of culture or standing up for what is right in the face of opposition. But when we are grounded in the truth of God's Word, we are able to stand firm in our convictions, knowing that we are standing on a solid foundation. We are called to stand for the truth of the gospel, to proclaim the good news of Jesus Christ, and to live out our faith in a way that reflects God's love and holiness to the world around us. This kind of standing is not about being combative or judgmental—it's about standing firm in the truth with love, grace, and humility, trusting that God's truth will ultimately prevail.

Standing firm in the truth also means standing in the face of personal trials and difficulties. There will be times in our lives when we are faced with challenges that shake us to our core—whether it's a health crisis, a financial struggle, a broken relationship, or a deep disappointment. In these moments, it can be tempting to give in to fear, doubt, or despair. But when we are girded with the truth of God's Word, we are able to stand firm, even in the midst of these trials. We know that God is with us, that He is for us, and that He will never abandon us. We know that He is working all things together for our good, even when we can't see it (Romans 8:28). Standing in the truth means trusting that God's promises are true, even when our circumstances make it difficult to believe. It means holding on to hope, even when everything around us feels uncertain. It means standing in faith, knowing that God is faithful and that He will carry us through whatever trials we face.

To stand firm in the truth also means standing in our identity as children of God. The world will try to define us by our achievements, our failures, or the opinions of others. But when we stand in the truth of God's Word, we are reminded that our identity is not found in what we do or what others think of us—it is found in who God says we are. We are His beloved children, redeemed by the blood of Jesus, and nothing can change that. This truth gives us the strength to stand firm in our faith, knowing that we are secure in God's love and grace. When we stand in this truth, we are able to live with confidence, knowing that our worth and value are not determined by the standards of this world, but by the unchanging love of our Heavenly Father.

Standing with our loins girt about with truth also means standing together as the body of Christ. We are not called to stand alone in this battle—God has given us the gift of community, the church, to stand alongside us. When we stand together, we are stronger. We encourage one another, support one another, and remind one another of the truth of God's Word. We are called to stand in unity, bearing one another's burdens, and helping each other remain steadfast in the faith. Standing firm in the truth as a community allows us to face the challenges of life with greater strength, knowing that we are not alone in this journey. Together, we can stand firm in the truth of the gospel, proclaiming it to the world and living it out in our daily lives.

As you continue through "Answer the Call – 31 Days of Bold Biblical Action", let this call to stand firm in the truth be an invitation to root yourself deeply in God's Word. If there are areas of your life where you have been swayed by doubt, fear, or the opinions of others, now is the time to anchor yourself in the truth of Scripture. Gird your loins with the truth of God's promises, and stand firm in the knowledge that His Word is unchanging, reliable, and powerful. Stand firm in your faith, trusting that God is with you, that He is for you, and that He will never leave you or forsake you.

Stand therefore, having your loins girt about with truth, and watch as God strengthens you, equips you, and gives you the courage to stand firm in the midst of any battle you may face. Stand firm in the truth of who God is, and stand firm in the truth of who you are in Him. Stand firm in the face of spiritual warfare, knowing that God has already won the victory through Jesus Christ. Stand firm in the truth, and be a light to a world that desperately needs to see the love, grace, and truth of God. Stand therefore, and experience the peace, confidence, and strength that come from being grounded in the unshakable truth of God's Word. Stand firm, and know that God is faithful, that His truth will never fail, and that He will carry you through every trial, every battle, and every challenge you face.

Chapter 14 – Repent

In the fourteenth call to action from "Answer the Call – 31 Days of Bold Biblical Action", we are faced with the powerful and transformative command found in Acts 3:19: "Repent ye therefore, and be converted, that your sins may be blotted out, when the times of refreshing shall come from the presence of the Lord;" These words from Scripture are not merely a suggestion; they are an urgent invitation to experience the radical change that comes from turning away from sin and turning toward God. To repent is to recognize that we have been walking down the wrong path, living in ways that are contrary to God's will, and it is to make a conscious decision to turn around—to turn away from our sins, our selfishness, and our rebellion, and to turn toward God's grace, forgiveness, and love. Repentance is not simply feeling sorry for our mistakes; it is a deep, heart-level transformation where we acknowledge the weight of our sin and realize that we cannot save ourselves. It is the recognition that we are broken, that we have fallen short of God's perfect standard, and that we need His mercy and grace to be made whole. But repentance doesn't end with sorrow—it leads to joy, because when we repent, we open the door to God's healing, forgiveness, and the new life that He offers us through Jesus Christ.

Repentance is the first step toward conversion, the turning point in our lives where everything changes. When we repent, we are choosing to leave behind the old way of life—our old habits, our old patterns of sin, our old way of thinking—and we are embracing the new life that God offers us in Christ. This is what it means to be converted: to be transformed by the power of God's grace, to be made new, and to begin walking in the light of His truth. Conversion is not just about a change in behavior; it's about a change in heart. It's about allowing God to reshape us from the inside out, to remove the guilt and shame that have weighed us down, and to replace them with His love, peace, and joy. When we repent and are converted, we are no longer defined by our past mistakes or sins—we are defined by God's grace. We become new creations in Christ (2 Corinthians 5:17), no longer bound by the chains of sin, but free to live in the fullness of life that God has for us.

But repentance is not always easy. It requires humility, honesty, and a willingness to admit that we have been wrong. It requires us to come face to face with the reality of our sin and to acknowledge that we need God's forgiveness. In a world that often encourages us to follow our own desires and to do whatever feels good in the moment, repentance calls us to a higher standard—it calls us to live according to God's truth, not according to our own. Repentance is an act of surrender, where we lay down our pride, our stubbornness, and our attempts to control our own lives, and we choose to trust God instead. This surrender is not a sign of weakness; it is a sign of strength, because it is only when we surrender to God that we can truly experience the freedom and peace that come from being in right relationship with Him.

One of the most beautiful aspects of repentance is that it leads to forgiveness. In Acts 3:19, Peter calls the people to repent so that their sins may be wiped away. When we repent, God doesn't hold our sins against us—He forgives them completely, washing us clean and removing them as far as the east is from the west (Psalm 103:12). This is the incredible gift of God's grace: no matter how far we've strayed, no matter how many mistakes we've made, when we repent, God forgives us and welcomes us back into His arms. He doesn't condemn us for our failures—He offers us mercy and a fresh start. This forgiveness is not something we can earn; it is a gift that God gives freely because of His great love for us. When we repent, we are met not with judgment, but with grace. We are met not with rejection, but with acceptance. God's forgiveness is total and complete, and it allows us to walk forward in newness of life, free from the guilt and shame of our past.

Repentance is not just a one-time act—it is a daily posture of the heart. As believers, we are called to live lives of continual repentance, where we are constantly turning away from sin and turning toward God. This doesn't mean that we are constantly living in fear of making mistakes, but rather that we are living with a heart that is open to God's correction and guidance. It means being sensitive to the Holy Spirit's conviction when we have strayed from God's path, and being quick to repent when we realize we have sinned. Repentance is a lifestyle of humility and dependence on God, where we recognize that we need His grace every day to live the way He has called us to live. It's about being willing to let go of anything in our lives that is not in line with God's will, and to continually seek His forgiveness, guidance, and strength to live in obedience to Him.

But repentance is not just about turning away from sin—it's about turning toward something better. When we repent, we are not just leaving behind our old way of life; we are stepping into the abundant life that God has for us. Repentance opens the door to a deeper relationship with God, where we experience His love, His presence, and His peace in new and profound ways. It allows us to walk in the freedom that comes from knowing that we are forgiven, loved, and accepted by God. When we repent and are converted, we are no longer living for ourselves—we are living for God, and our lives take on a new sense of purpose and meaning. Repentance is not about giving up something good; it's about exchanging something broken for something beautiful. It's about trading the lies of sin for the truth of God's Word, and the emptiness of the world for the fullness of life in Christ.

Repentance is also the doorway to healing. Many of us carry deep wounds—whether they are emotional, spiritual, or relational—that have been caused by our own sins or the sins of others. These wounds can weigh us down, keeping us trapped in cycles of pain, bitterness, or guilt. But when we repent, we invite God's healing power into those broken places. We give Him access to the parts of our hearts that have been hurt, and we allow Him to bring restoration and wholeness. Repentance is the first step toward healing, because it is in repentance that we acknowledge our need for God's grace and invite Him to work in our lives. When we repent, we are not just forgiven—we are made whole. God takes the broken pieces of our lives and puts them back together in a way that only He can, bringing beauty from the ashes of our past mistakes.

In addition to personal healing, repentance leads to reconciliation. Sin often creates division—between us and God, and between us and others. When we live in sin, it not only affects our relationship with God, but it also damages our relationships with the people around us. But repentance has the power to restore what has been broken. When we repent, we are reconciled to God, and we are also called to seek reconciliation with others. Repentance humbles us, softens our hearts, and allows us to take responsibility for the ways we have hurt others. It gives us the courage to ask for forgiveness and to extend forgiveness to those who have hurt us. Through repentance, relationships can be healed, wounds can be mended, and unity can be restored. This is the power of repentance: it not only transforms our hearts, but it also transforms our relationships, bringing peace, healing, and restoration where there was once division and pain.

Repentance is also a powerful witness to the world. When people see the transformation that comes from a heart that has repented and been converted, they are drawn to the hope and grace of the gospel. Our lives become a testimony to the power of God's love and forgiveness. When we live lives of repentance, we are not hiding our mistakes or pretending to be perfect—we are openly acknowledging our need for God's grace and showing others the freedom that comes from being forgiven. This kind of humility and honesty is rare in a world that often values self-sufficiency and pride, but it is deeply attractive because it points people to the only One who can truly save and heal. Our repentance is not just for our own benefit—it is a way for us to share the good news of the gospel with others, inviting them to experience the same forgiveness and transformation that we have found in Christ.

As you continue through "Answer the Call – 31 Days of Bold Biblical Action", let this call to repent be an invitation to experience the freedom, healing, and transformation that come from turning away from sin and turning toward God. If there are areas in your life where you have been holding on to sin, now is the time to repent and be converted. Don't wait—God is ready and willing to forgive you, to cleanse you, and to give you a fresh start. Repentance is not something to be feared—it is a gift of God's grace, an opportunity to be made new and to walk in the fullness of life that He has for you.

Repent ye therefore, and be converted, and watch as God takes your brokenness and turns it into something beautiful. Repent, and experience the joy of knowing that your sins are forgiven, your past is washed away, and you are a new creation in Christ. Repent, and step into the abundant life that God has prepared for you—a life filled with His love, peace, and purpose. Repent, and be healed, be restored, and be reconciled to God and to those around you. Repent, and let your life be a testimony to the power of God's grace and the transforming work of His Spirit. Repent, and watch as God makes all things new.

Chapter 15 – Go

In the fifteenth call to action from "Answer the Call – 31 Days of Bold Biblical Action", we are given one of the most powerful and urgent commands from Jesus: "Go ye therefore, and teach all nations, baptizing them in the name of the Father, and of the Son, and of the Holy Ghost:" (Matthew 28:19). These words, known as the Great Commission, were among the final instructions Jesus gave to His disciples before He ascended into heaven, and they carry a weight of eternal significance. Jesus wasn't simply telling His disciples to go on a journey or to visit foreign lands—He was calling them, and by extension, calling us, to a mission that transcends geography, culture, and time. He was inviting us to participate in the most important work in the world: sharing the good news of His love, grace, and salvation with every person, everywhere. The word "Go" is a command, not a suggestion. It's a call to action, a call to step out of our comfort zones, and to take the gospel to the ends of the earth. This command is not just for pastors, missionaries, or evangelists—it is for every believer. We are all called to go, to share the gospel, and to make disciples of all nations. The Great Commission is a reminder that the gospel is not something to be kept to ourselves; it is a message that is meant to be shared, a message of hope, life, and redemption that has the power to transform hearts, communities, and entire nations.

To "Go" means to be active in our faith. It means that we cannot be content to simply sit in church on Sundays, listen to sermons, and go about our daily lives without engaging with the world around us. Jesus calls us to be His witnesses, to share His message of love and salvation with others, and to make disciples. This doesn't necessarily mean that we are all called to travel to distant countries, although for some, that may be the case. "Going" can happen right where we are—at work, in our schools, in our neighborhoods, and even in our homes. Jesus' command to "Go" is about a mindset, a heart posture that is ready and willing to share the gospel wherever we are, with whoever God places in our path. It's about living with intentionality, always looking for opportunities to share the love of Christ with others. When we take this command seriously, we begin to see every interaction, every conversation, and every relationship as an opportunity to point people to Jesus.

The call to "Go" is also a call to trust in God's power and provision. When Jesus gave the Great Commission, He didn't expect His disciples to accomplish it in their own strength. In fact, before He told them to go, He reminded them of His authority: "All power is given unto me in heaven and in earth" (Matthew 28:18). Jesus was assuring His disciples that He had all the authority and power they would need to fulfill the mission. And in the next verse, He promised to be with them always, even to the end of the world (Matthew 28:20). This promise is for us too. When we go, we don't go alone—we go in the power of Jesus and with the assurance of His presence. He is with us every step of the way, guiding us, equipping us, and giving us the courage to share His message with the world. The task of reaching the nations can feel overwhelming, but we can take comfort in knowing that it is God who is at work through us. We are simply the vessels He uses to accomplish His purposes.

Going and teaching all nations means sharing the full gospel—proclaiming the message of Jesus' life, death, and resurrection, and inviting people into a relationship with Him. It's not just about giving people information; it's about leading them to a place of transformation. Jesus didn't call us to make converts—He called us to make disciples. This means walking alongside people as they grow in their faith, helping them to understand who Jesus is, what He has done for them, and what it means to follow Him. Making disciples requires time, patience, and love. It's about investing in others, teaching them to obey everything Jesus has commanded, and helping them become followers of Jesus who will, in turn, make more disciples. This process of disciple-making is how the gospel spreads and how the church grows. It's a multiplication process—one person shares the gospel with another, who then shares it with someone else, and the message of Jesus continues to spread across the world.

But going and making disciples is not without challenges. There will be times when we face rejection, opposition, or even persecution for sharing our faith. Jesus warned His disciples that the world would not always accept the message of the gospel, and that following Him would come with a cost (John

15:18-20). But He also reminded them that the reward far outweighs the cost. When we go, we are participating in the most important work in the world—the work of bringing people into the kingdom of God. Every time we share the gospel, every time we make a disciple, we are contributing to something that has eternal significance. The souls of the people we reach will live forever, either with God in heaven or separated from Him in hell. This is why the Great Commission is so urgent. We are called to go because eternity is at stake.

One of the most powerful aspects of Jesus' command to "Go" is that it is inclusive. He tells us to go to "all nations," meaning that the gospel is for everyone, regardless of race, culture, language, or background. There is no one who is beyond the reach of God's love. The Great Commission breaks down all barriers and reminds us that God's heart is for the whole world. He desires that every person, in every corner of the earth, hear the good news of Jesus Christ and have the opportunity to respond to it. This means that we are called to cross boundaries—whether they are physical, cultural, or relational—to bring the gospel to those who have never heard it. It means being willing to step out of our comfort zones and engage with people who may be different from us. It means seeing the world through God's eyes and recognizing that every person we meet is someone for whom Christ died.

The command to "Go" also reminds us that the gospel is not just for certain types of people. It's not just for the religious, the morally upright, or the people who seem like they have their lives together. The gospel is for the broken, the lost, the hurting, and the outcast. It's for the people who feel like they are too far gone, who think that God could never love them, and who believe that there is no hope for their lives. When Jesus tells us to go and make disciples of all nations, He is calling us to reach out to the least, the last, and the lost. He is calling us to share His love with those who have been forgotten or overlooked by the world. The gospel is the message of hope that every person needs, and it is our responsibility to take that message to those who are in desperate need of it.

As we respond to Jesus' command to "Go," we must also be prepared to go with love and compassion. Sharing the gospel is not about winning arguments or forcing people to believe what we believe. It's about loving people enough to tell them the truth and to invite them into a relationship with the God who created them and loves them. It's about showing people the love of Jesus through our actions, our words, and our lives. When we go and make disciples, we are not just telling people about Jesus—we are showing them who He is by the way we live. We are called to be ambassadors of Christ, representing Him to the world, and showing people what it looks like to follow Him. This means that our lives must reflect the love, grace, and truth of the gospel. It means living in such a way that people see Jesus in us and are drawn to Him through our witness.

Going and making disciples is a lifelong mission. It's not something we do once and then move on from—it's a calling that we carry with us for the rest of our lives. Every day, we have opportunities to share the gospel, to make disciples, and to participate in the Great Commission. Whether we are sharing the gospel with a coworker, discipling a new believer, or supporting missionaries who are taking the gospel to unreached people groups, we are fulfilling the call to "Go." This mission is not limited by our circumstances or our location. No matter where we are or what season of life we are in, we can be part of God's mission to reach the world with the good news of Jesus Christ.

As you continue through "Answer the Call – 31 Days of Bold Biblical Action", let this call to "Go" be an invitation to step into the mission that God has for you. If you have been hesitant to share your faith, or if you have been waiting for the right moment to get involved in the Great Commission, now is the time to go. The world is full of people who are waiting to hear the good news of Jesus Christ, and God is calling you to be His messenger. You don't have to have all the answers or be perfect—you just have to be willing to go. Trust that God will give you the words, the courage, and the opportunities to share His love with others. Go with confidence, knowing that Jesus has all authority and that He is with you every step of the way.

Go, and teach all nations. Go, and make disciples. Go, and share the love, grace, and truth of Jesus Christ with a world that desperately needs to know Him. This is the mission that God has entrusted to each of us, and it is a mission that has eternal significance. Go, and watch as God works through you to transform hearts, lives, and communities. Go, and be

part of the incredible story that God is writing—a story of redemption, hope, and salvation for all who believe. Go, and experience the joy and fulfillment that come from living out the Great Commission, knowing that you are participating in the most important work in the world. Go, and let your life be a testimony to the power of the gospel and the love of Jesus Christ. Go, and see how God can use you to change the world, one life at a time.

Chapter 16 – Teach

In the sixteenth call to action from "Answer the Call – 31 Days of Bold Biblical Action", we encounter the profound command given by Jesus in Matthew 28:20: "Teaching them to observe all things whatsoever I have commanded you: and, lo, I am with you alway, even unto the end of the world. Amen." These words are part of the Great Commission, where Jesus instructs His disciples to go into all the world and make disciples of all nations. However, this call to "teach" goes far beyond simply spreading knowledge or delivering sermons—it's a call to invest in others' lives, to guide them, and to help them live out the truths of the gospel in their everyday lives. Jesus didn't just tell His disciples to preach; He told them to teach, to walk alongside people, and to show them how to observe and obey everything He had commanded. This is a call to discipleship—a lifelong process of helping others grow in their faith, understand God's Word, and live out the teachings of Jesus in every area of their lives. Teaching, in this sense, is not just about transferring information—it's about transformation. It's about leading people into a deeper relationship with God, helping them apply His truth to their lives, and equipping them to live as faithful followers of Christ.

When Jesus says, "teaching them to observe all things," He's calling us to more than just head knowledge. He's calling us to teach others how to live a life of obedience to God, how to walk in faith, and how to follow Him with their whole hearts. The goal of teaching in the context of the Great Commission is not just to help people know more about Jesus, but to help them become more like Jesus. It's about teaching people to live according to the Word of God, to obey His commandments, and to reflect His character in their actions, attitudes, and relationships. This kind of teaching requires patience, love, and a deep commitment to seeing others grow spiritually. It's about coming alongside people in their journey of faith and helping them navigate the challenges and joys of following Christ.

Teaching others to observe all things is also about modeling the Christian life. We can't just tell people what to do—we have to show them what it looks like to live out the gospel. This means that our lives must be a reflection of the teachings of Jesus. We are called to be living examples of what it means to follow Christ, to love others as He loved, to serve with humility, and to walk in obedience to God's commands. Teaching others to observe all things requires us to live with integrity, to be consistent in our faith, and to practice what we preach. People are not just listening to our words; they are watching how we live. If we want to teach others to observe all things, we must first be committed to observing those things ourselves. Our lives must reflect the truth of the gospel, so that when people see us, they see a glimpse of Jesus.

But teaching others to observe all things is not just about our example—it's also about coming alongside others with intentionality and care. It's about building relationships, investing in people's lives, and walking with them through the ups and downs of their faith journey. Teaching in the context of discipleship is not a one-time event; it's a long-term commitment to helping others grow. It involves listening to their struggles, answering their questions, and encouraging them when they feel discouraged. It's about being there for them in the difficult moments and celebrating with them in the moments of victory. True discipleship is relational—it's about walking together in community, helping each other grow, and holding one another accountable to live according to God's Word.

Teaching others to observe all things also requires us to be deeply rooted in God's Word. We cannot teach what we do not know. If we are going to teach others to follow Jesus, we must first be students of His Word ourselves. This means spending time in Scripture, studying His teachings, and applying His truth to our own lives. It means being committed to learning and growing in our own faith, so that we can effectively teach others. We must be people who are hungry for God's Word, who are constantly seeking to know Him more, and who are willing to submit our lives to His authority. When we are grounded in the truth of Scripture, we are equipped to teach others, to help them understand the Word of God, and to show them how to live it out in their daily lives.

One of the most beautiful aspects of teaching others to observe all things is that it is a process of multiplication. When we teach others to follow Jesus, we are equipping them to go and teach others as well. Discipleship is a multiplication process—one person teaches another, who then teaches another, and the gospel continues to spread. This is how the church grows, how the kingdom of God expands, and how the Great Commission is fulfilled. Jesus didn't just call us to make converts—He called us to make disciples. And making disciples means teaching them to observe all that He has commanded. This process of teaching and disciple-making is how the gospel reaches the ends of the earth. It's not about one person doing it all—it's about each of us playing our part, investing in the lives of others, and helping them grow in their faith so that they can go and do the same for others.

But teaching others to observe all things is not without challenges. There will be times when people are resistant to the teachings of Jesus, when they struggle to understand or accept His commands. There will be moments when people fall short, when they make mistakes, or when they doubt their faith. In these moments, we are called to teach with patience, grace, and love. We are called to walk with people through their struggles, to encourage them to keep going, and to remind them of God's grace and forgiveness. Teaching others to observe all things requires us to be patient and persistent, knowing that spiritual growth is a process and that God is at work in people's lives even when we don't see immediate results. It's about trusting that God's Word will not return void, but will accomplish the purpose for which it was sent (Isaiah 55:11).

Another important aspect of teaching others to observe all things is that it involves teaching the whole counsel of God. Jesus didn't say, "Teach them to observe some things"—He said, "Teach them to observe all things." This means that we are called to teach the full truth of God's Word, not just the parts that are easy or comfortable. There may be times when teaching the truth of Scripture is difficult, when it challenges people's beliefs or confronts their sin. But we are called to be faithful to God's Word, to teach it in its entirety, and to trust that God will use His truth to bring conviction, transformation, and growth. Teaching others to observe all things means teaching both the comforting promises of God and the hard truths that call us to repentance and obedience. It means teaching about God's love, grace, and forgiveness, as well as

His holiness, justice, and righteousness. We must be faithful to teach the whole gospel, trusting that God's Word is powerful and able to transform lives.

Teaching others to observe all things is also about equipping people to live out their faith in practical ways. It's about helping them apply the truths of Scripture to their everyday lives, whether it's in their relationships, their work, their decisions, or their struggles. Teaching others to observe all things is about giving them the tools they need to live as faithful followers of Jesus in a world that often pulls them in the opposite direction. It's about teaching them how to pray, how to read and study the Bible, how to share their faith, and how to serve others. It's about helping them develop spiritual disciplines and habits that will strengthen their faith and keep them grounded in God's truth. This kind of teaching is practical, relational, and focused on helping people grow in their relationship with God and live out their faith in the real world.

Teaching others to observe all things is a high calling, but it is also one that is filled with joy and fulfillment. There is nothing more rewarding than seeing someone grow in their faith, watching them come to a deeper understanding of God's Word, and witnessing the transformation that takes place in their lives as they follow Jesus. When we invest in others through teaching and discipleship, we are participating in God's work of transforming hearts and building His kingdom. We are helping others experience the abundant life that Jesus came to give, and we are playing a part in the fulfillment of the Great Commission. Teaching others to observe all things is not just about what we can give—it's also about what we receive. As we teach, we are often the ones who are most blessed, as we see God at work in the lives of others and experience the joy of being used by Him to make a difference in the world.

As you continue through "Answer the Call – 31 Days of Bold Biblical Action", let this call to teach be an invitation to invest in the lives of others, to disciple them, and to help them grow in their faith. If you feel inadequate or unsure about your ability to teach, remember that God is the one who equips us for the work He calls us to do. You don't have to be a Bible scholar or a seasoned teacher to disciple someone—you just have to be willing to share what you have learned and to walk alongside others in their journey of faith. Trust that God will use you, that He will give you the wisdom and words you need, and that He will work through you to make disciples.

Teach others to observe all things, and watch as God works through you to transform lives and build His kingdom. Teach with love, with patience, and with a heart that is committed to helping others grow in their relationship with Jesus. Teach the full truth of God's Word, trusting that His truth has the power to change hearts and lives. Teach with intentionality, building relationships and investing in others' lives, knowing that discipleship is a lifelong process of

growth and transformation. Teach, and be part of the incredible mission that Jesus has given us—to make disciples of all nations, teaching them to observe all that He has commanded. Teach, and experience the joy of seeing others come to know Jesus, grow in their faith, and live out the teachings of the gospel in their daily lives. Teach, and watch as God uses your efforts to impact the world for His glory.

Chapter 17 – Cast

In the seventeenth call to action from "Answer the Call – 31 Days of Bold Biblical Action", we encounter one of the most comforting and deeply emotional instructions in Scripture: "Casting all your care upon him; for he careth for you." (1 Peter 5:7). These words are like a warm embrace for the weary soul, a reminder that no matter how heavy our burdens may feel, no matter how overwhelming life becomes, we are not alone in carrying them. To "cast" our cares upon God is more than simply praying about our problems or thinking about giving them to Him; it is an intentional, wholehearted act of surrender. It's the moment we realize that the weight we have been carrying—whether it be anxiety, fear, stress, heartache, or worry—is too much for us to bear on our own. And in that moment of surrender, we place it all at the feet of the One who is not only capable of carrying it but who actually invites us to give it to Him. The word "cast" suggests throwing something off of ourselves, tossing it away from us entirely. God doesn't want us to hold on to our burdens, to carry them day after day, weighed down by the cares of this world. He is calling us to release them into His hands, to trust Him fully with every fear, every doubt, every stress, and every sorrow that weighs on our hearts.

This verse speaks to the very core of our human experience—the reality that life is often filled with cares, worries, and struggles that can leave us feeling anxious, overwhelmed, or even hopeless. But the beauty of this command is found in the reason for our casting: "for He careth for you." This simple yet profound truth—that the God of the universe cares for us personally—changes everything. It means that we don't have to face life's challenges alone. It means that the God who created the heavens and the earth, the One who holds all power in His hands, deeply cares about the details of our lives. He sees every tear, hears every anxious thought, and understands every fear we carry in our hearts. And because He cares for us, He invites us to come to Him with all of it.

There is no burden too small, no worry too insignificant, and no problem too big for God to handle. He is not indifferent to our struggles—He cares about them, and He cares about us. This is the heart of the gospel: that God, in His infinite love, invites us into a relationship where we can cast all our cares on Him and trust that He will take care of us.

Casting our cares upon God requires trust—trust that He is good, that He is capable, and that He truly cares for us. It's one thing to know intellectually that God cares for us, but it's another thing entirely to trust Him enough to release our worries and fears into His hands. Often, we try to hold on to our burdens, thinking that we need to figure everything out on our own or that we need to be strong enough to handle life's challenges. But God doesn't ask us to carry these burdens by ourselves. In fact, He tells us that we weren't meant to. Jesus Himself invites us to come to Him when we are weary and burdened, promising to give us rest (Matthew 11:28). Casting our cares on God is an act of faith—it's choosing to trust that He will take care of the things that are weighing us down, even when we can't see how He's going to do it. It's about letting go of the illusion of control and trusting that God is sovereign over every detail of our lives.

But casting our cares on God doesn't mean that our problems will instantly disappear. It doesn't mean that life will suddenly become easy or that we won't face challenges anymore. What it does mean is that we don't have to face those challenges alone. It means that we have a loving, all-powerful God who is walking with us every step of the way, carrying the burdens that we cannot carry on our own. It means that we can rest in the assurance that God is working behind the scenes, even when we can't see it. He is working all things together for our good (Romans 8:28), and He is faithful to provide for our needs, guide our steps, and strengthen us in our weakness. Casting our cares on God is about finding peace in the midst of the storm, knowing that our burdens are in the hands of the One who can handle them far better than we ever could.

One of the most beautiful aspects of this verse is the personal nature of God's care for us. It's not just that God cares about humanity in general—He cares about you, specifically. He knows your name, your story, your fears, and your hopes. He knows what keeps you up at night, what weighs on your heart, and what burdens you carry. And He invites you, personally, to cast all of that onto Him. This is the heart of a loving Father who wants to care for His children, not from a distance, but in a deeply personal and intimate way. God doesn't want us to struggle under the weight of our burdens alone—He wants to walk with us through them, to carry the weight for us, and to give us peace in the midst of our struggles.

To cast our cares upon God also means to release the need to have all the answers. So often, our worries and anxieties stem from trying to figure out how everything will work out—how we'll solve a problem, how we'll overcome a challenge, how we'll make it through a difficult situation. But when we cast our cares on God, we are releasing the need to have all the answers, and we are trusting that God already has them. We are acknowledging that His wisdom is greater than ours, that His plans are better than ours, and that He is in control. This kind of trust brings freedom—freedom from the constant pressure to have it all figured out, freedom from the anxiety of not knowing what's going to happen, and freedom to rest in the knowledge that God is working on our behalf.

Casting our cares upon God also means surrendering our worries about the future. So much of our anxiety comes from worrying about things that haven't even happened yet—about the "what ifs" and the unknowns of the future. But God calls us to trust Him with the future, knowing that He holds it in His hands. Jesus Himself told us not to worry about tomorrow, for tomorrow will worry about itself (Matthew 6:34). When we cast our cares on God, we are choosing to live in the present, trusting that God will provide for us today and that He will take care of the future when it comes. We are choosing to rest in His provision, His protection, and His perfect timing. This doesn't mean that we don't plan or think about the future—it means that we don't let the uncertainties of the future steal the peace that God offers us today.

Casting our cares on God also allows us to experience His peace. When we hold on to our worries, our hearts and minds are often filled with anxiety, fear, and stress. But when we release those worries to God, we make room for His peace to fill our hearts. Philippians 4:6-7 reminds us that when we bring our requests to God with thanksgiving, His peace, which surpasses all understanding, will guard our hearts and minds in Christ Jesus. This peace is not dependent on our circumstances—it's a peace that comes from knowing that God is in control, that He cares for us, and that He is working all things for our good. When we cast our cares on God, we are trading our anxiety for His peace, our fear for His comfort, and our stress for His rest.

But casting our cares on God is not something we do once and then move on from—it's a continual process. Life is full of cares and burdens that come at us daily, and each time they arise, we are invited to cast them on God once again. This is a daily act of surrender, a daily choice to trust God with the things that weigh us down. It's about developing a habit of turning to God with every worry, every fear, and every burden, knowing that He is always there, ready to take them from us. And as we make this a regular part of our lives, we grow in our trust in God, and we experience more of His peace and presence in our daily lives.

As you continue through "Answer the Call – 31 Days of Bold Biblical Action", let this call to cast your cares upon God be an invitation to release the burdens you've been carrying and to trust in His care for you. If there are worries, fears, or anxieties that have been weighing on your heart, now is the time to cast them on God. He is inviting you to let go of the things that are too heavy for you to carry, and to trust that He will take care of them for you. Don't hold on to your burdens any longer—cast them on the One who cares for you, who loves you, and who is more than able to handle whatever you are facing.

Cast all your cares upon Him, and experience the freedom that comes from releasing your worries into His hands. Cast your cares upon Him, and feel the weight lifted from your shoulders as God takes your burdens and carries them for you. Cast your cares upon Him, and know that He cares deeply for you—that He sees you, loves you, and is working all things together for your good. Cast your cares upon Him, and rest in the assurance that you are not alone, that you are held by a loving Father who is always with you, always for you, and always ready to help you. Cast your cares upon Him, and experience the peace, comfort, and strength that come from trusting in the One who holds all things in His hands.

Chapter 18 – Worship

In the eighteenth call to action from "Answer the Call – 31 Days of Bold Biblical Action", we come to one of the most profound commands in all of Scripture: "Then saith Jesus unto him, Get thee hence, Satan: for it is written, Thou shalt worship the Lord thy God, and him only shalt thou serve." (Matthew 4:10). This command goes to the very core of who we are as human beings and what our ultimate purpose is in life. We were created to worship—to adore, to reverence, and to glorify the One who made us. Worship is not just an action; it is a state of being, a posture of the heart that acknowledges the greatness, holiness, and majesty of God. It is the natural response of a soul that has encountered the living God, the Creator of heaven and earth, the Savior who has redeemed us, and the King who reigns over all. To worship God is to place Him at the very center of our lives, to honor Him with every thought, word, and action, and to live in awe of His goodness, grace, and power. True worship flows from a heart that recognizes its utter dependence on God, its need for His mercy and grace, and its deep desire to know and love Him more fully. Worship is not something we do for God; it is something we offer to Him out of gratitude and love for all that He is and all that He has done for us.

When Jesus says, "Thou shalt worship the Lord thy God," He is calling us to a life of worship, a life that is centered on Him and His glory. Worship is more than singing songs or attending church services—it is a lifestyle. It is about living in constant awareness of God's presence and seeking to honor Him in everything we do. Worship happens when we choose to praise God in the midst of both joy and pain, when we trust Him in times of uncertainty, and when we live in obedience to His Word. Worship is not confined to a specific place or time; it is something we carry with us wherever we go. It's about recognizing that every moment of our lives is an opportunity to glorify God—to reflect His love, His goodness, and His truth to the world around us. This is why Jesus emphasized that true worshipers will worship the Father in spirit and in truth (John 4:23). It's not about rituals or outward displays of piety—it's about the posture of our hearts before God.

At its core, worship is an act of surrender. To worship God is to acknowledge that He is Lord of our lives, that He is in control, and that we belong to Him. It's about laying down our own desires, ambitions, and plans, and submitting to His will. True worship requires humility, because it means recognizing that God is infinitely greater than we are, and that our lives are not our own—they are His. This kind of surrender is not always easy, especially in a world that encourages us to seek our own way, to pursue our own goals, and to live for ourselves. But worship calls us to something higher—it calls us to live for God's glory, to seek first His kingdom and His righteousness, and to trust that He will take care of the rest (Matthew 6:33). When we worship God, we are declaring that He is worthy of our trust, our love, and our obedience, and we are choosing to live for His purposes rather than our own.

Worship is also a response to God's love. The Bible tells us that we love because He first loved us (1 John 4:19). Our worship is a response to the incredible love that God has poured out on us through His Son, Jesus Christ. When we think about the sacrifice that Jesus made for us—how He left the glory of heaven, took on human flesh, and gave His life on the cross to save us from our sins—how can we not respond in worship? Worship is our way of saying, "Thank You, Lord, for saving me. Thank You for loving me when I was unworthy. Thank You for giving me new life and hope." It is the overflow of a heart that has been touched by God's grace and transformed by His love. Worship is not about us—it's about God. It's about magnifying His name, lifting Him up, and declaring His greatness to the world.

Worship also reminds us of who God is. In a world that is constantly changing, where we face uncertainty, trials, and challenges, worship centers us on the unchanging character of God. It reminds us that He is faithful, that He is good, that He is sovereign over all, and that He never fails. When we worship, we are reminding ourselves of the truth that God is in control, even when life feels out of control. Worship helps us to shift our focus from our circumstances to the greatness of God. It reminds us that no matter what we are going through, God is with us, He is for us, and He is working all things together for our good (Romans 8:28). Worship gives us perspective—it lifts our eyes from the temporal struggles of this life and fixes them on the eternal promises of God.

One of the most beautiful aspects of worship is that it brings us into the presence of God. The Bible tells us that God inhabits the praises of His people (Psalm 22:3). When we worship, we are inviting God to come and dwell among us, to meet us in a personal and powerful way. Worship is not just something we do for God—it is a time when we encounter Him, when we experience His presence, His peace, and His love. In worship, we are reminded that God is not distant or far off—He is near to us, and He desires to have a relationship with us. Worship is a time when we can pour out our hearts to God, when we can bring our fears, our struggles, and our burdens to Him, and when we can receive His comfort and strength. In worship, we are reminded that we are not alone—that the God of the universe is with us, and that He cares deeply about every detail of our lives.

Worship is also a declaration of faith. When we worship God, we are declaring that we believe in His promises, that we trust in His Word, and that we are confident in His plan for our lives. Even when we don't understand what God is doing, even when life doesn't make sense, worship is a way of saying, "Lord, I trust You. I believe that You are good, and I know that You are working all things for my good." Worship strengthens our faith because it reminds us of God's faithfulness in the past and gives us hope for the future. It helps us to cling to the promises of God, even when we are walking through the darkest valleys. Worship is a way of standing firm in our faith, of refusing to be shaken by the storms of life, and of holding on to the truth that God is with us, and He will never leave us or forsake us.

But worship is not just about what we receive—it's about what we give. Worship is an offering that we bring to God. It is an act of giving Him the honor, glory, and praise that He deserves. The Bible tells us to present our bodies as a living sacrifice, holy and acceptable to God, which is our reasonable act of worship (Romans 12:1). Worship is about offering our whole selves—our hearts, our minds, our bodies, our time, our talents—to God in service to Him. It's about living a life that reflects His love and His truth. True worship is not confined to a church service; it is a way of life. It's about how we live every day—how we treat others, how we spend our time, how we use our resources, and how we pursue God's will for our lives. Worship is about giving God the best of ourselves, not just the leftovers. It's about putting Him first in everything we do and living in a way that honors Him.

Worship is also a source of strength. When we worship, we are reminded of God's power and His ability to do the impossible. In times of weakness, worship strengthens us by reminding us that we serve a God who is all-powerful, who can move mountains, and who can make a way where there seems to be no way. Worship lifts our spirits, renews our hope, and fills us with the joy of the Lord, which is our strength (Nehemiah 8:10). There is something powerful about praising God, even in the midst of difficulty. It shifts the atmosphere, it breaks chains, and it releases the power of God in our lives. Worship is not just a passive act—it is a weapon in spiritual warfare. When we worship, we are declaring victory in the name of Jesus over every fear, every obstacle, and every attack of the enemy.

In addition, worship unites us with other believers. When we come together in worship, we are reminded that we are part of something bigger than ourselves—we are part of the body of Christ. Worship brings us together as a community of faith, united in our love for God and our desire to glorify Him. It reminds us that we are not alone in our journey of faith—we have brothers and sisters in Christ who are walking alongside us, lifting us up in prayer, and encouraging us to keep going. Worship is a time when we come together to celebrate the goodness of God, to share in His love, and to strengthen one another in our faith. It is a beautiful picture of the unity and diversity of the body of Christ, as people from all backgrounds, cultures, and nations come together to worship the One true God.

As you continue through "Answer the Call – 31 Days of Bold Biblical Action", let this call to worship be an invitation to enter into a deeper, more intimate relationship with God. Worship is not something we do because we have to—it is something we do because we get to. It is a privilege and an honor to worship the God who created us, who loves us, and who has redeemed us through His Son, Jesus Christ. If there are areas of your life where you have been holding back, where you have not fully surrendered to God, let this be the moment when you offer them to Him in worship. Worship is about giving God your whole heart, your whole life, and trusting Him with every part of it.

Worship the Lord your God with all your heart, all your soul, and all your mind. Worship Him in spirit and in truth, and watch as He meets you in that place of surrender, as He fills you with His peace, His presence, and His love. Worship Him not just with your words, but with your life, offering yourself as a living sacrifice, holy and pleasing to Him. Worship Him in the good times and the hard times, knowing that He is worthy of all praise, and that He is working all things for your good.

Worship the Lord, and experience the joy, peace, and strength that come from being in His presence. Worship Him, and let your life be a testimony to His goodness, His grace, and His faithfulness. Worship Him, and know that He is with you, that He cares for you, and that He is worthy of all honor and glory. Worship the Lord your God, and live a life that brings glory to His name, for He alone is worthy of all praise.

Chapter 19 – Call

In the nineteenth call to action from "Answer the Call – 31 Days of Bold Biblical Action", we are invited into one of the most personal and comforting promises from God: "Call unto me, and I will answer thee, and shew thee great and mighty things, which thou knowest not." (Jeremiah 33:3). These words from God Himself are like a lifeline to every heart that has ever felt lost, overwhelmed, or uncertain. In this verse, God is extending an open invitation to each of us to call on Him, to bring our fears, questions, burdens, and even our doubts to Him, with the assurance that He will answer us. The word "call" is more than just a suggestion; it's a plea from a loving Father who longs to hear the cries of His children. It's an invitation into a relationship, a deep connection with the Creator of the universe who is not distant or unreachable but is near, ready, and eager to listen. When God says, "Call unto me," He is inviting us into the intimacy of prayer, into a conversation where we can pour out our hearts before Him, knowing that He is listening. He doesn't just promise to hear us; He promises to answer us. This is a divine guarantee that when we seek Him, we will find Him, when we call, He will respond, and when we cry out, He will show up in ways that go beyond our understanding.

To call on God is to acknowledge that we are not self-sufficient, that we cannot navigate life's challenges on our own, and that we need His guidance, strength, and wisdom. It's an act of humility, a recognition that we are dependent on Him. But it is also an act of faith, because when we call on God, we are trusting that He is who He says He is—the God who loves us, who is for us, and who is actively involved in every detail of our lives. This invitation to call on Him is not reserved for the righteous or those who have it all together—it's for everyone, no matter where they are in life. Whether we are in the midst of joy or sorrow, whether we are confident or confused, whether we are strong or broken, God's invitation to call on Him stands. It's an invitation for the weary soul to find rest, for the brokenhearted to find healing, for the anxious mind to find peace, and for the lost to find direction.

When God says, "Call unto me, and I will answer thee," He is offering us a relationship that is alive and active, not distant or passive. He is saying that He wants to be involved in our lives, that He cares about our struggles, our worries, and our hopes. He is not a God who is too busy or too far removed to hear us; He is the God who is intimately involved in every aspect of our lives. The promise that God will answer us is one of the most comforting assurances we can receive. It means that our prayers do not fall on deaf ears, that our cries for help are not ignored, and that our longing for direction and comfort is met with God's presence and response. His answer may not always come in the way we expect or in the timing we desire, but His promise is sure: He will answer. This assurance gives us the confidence to approach Him with boldness, knowing that we are not alone in our struggles, that He hears us, and that He will provide the guidance, strength, and peace that we need.

Calling on God is not just about presenting our requests to Him; it's about engaging in a relationship with Him. It's about drawing near to Him and experiencing the depth of His love, grace, and mercy. When we call on God, we are entering into a conversation with the One who knows us better than we know ourselves, who sees the things we cannot see, and who holds the future in His hands. This call to pray is an invitation to deeper intimacy with God, where we are not only asking for His help but also seeking to know Him more fully. Prayer is not just about getting answers; it's about growing in our relationship with God, learning to trust Him more, and experiencing His presence in our lives. When we call on God, we are opening our hearts to Him, inviting Him into the deepest parts of our souls, and allowing Him to work in ways that transform us from the inside out.

One of the most beautiful aspects of this promise is that it is personal. God is not just telling us to call on Him in a general sense; He is inviting you specifically to call on Him. He knows your name, your story, your struggles, and your dreams. He knows the burdens you carry, the fears that keep you awake at night, and the questions that weigh on your heart. And He is saying to you, "Call unto me, and I will answer you." This is a personal invitation from the God who created you, who loves you, and who wants to be intimately involved in your life. He doesn't just want you to call on Him in times of crisis—He wants you to call on Him in every moment of your life, to share your joys, your fears, your hopes, and your struggles with Him. He is not a distant, impersonal deity; He is your loving Father, your Savior, and your Friend.

Calling on God also reminds us that we are not in control, but that He is. So often, we try to handle life's challenges on our own, thinking that we need to figure everything out or carry the weight of the world on our shoulders. But when we call on God, we are acknowledging that He is the one who is truly in control, that He is sovereign over all things, and that He is more than capable of handling whatever we are facing. This act of calling on God is an act of surrender, where we lay down our burdens, our fears, and our need for control, and we place them in God's hands, trusting that He will take care of them. It's about releasing the things that are too heavy for us to carry and trusting that God will carry them for us. When we call on God, we are trusting that His ways are higher than our ways, that His plans are better than ours, and that He knows what is best for us, even when we don't understand.

But calling on God is not just something we do when we are in need—it's something we are invited to do continually. In 1 Thessalonians 5:17, we are told to "pray without ceasing," which means that calling on God is meant to be a constant part of our lives. It's not just about bringing our requests to Him once in a while; it's about living in a continual conversation with Him, where we are constantly turning our hearts and minds toward Him throughout the day. This kind of prayer is not about formal words or lengthy prayers—it's about a heart that is always in tune with God, a life that is lived in constant awareness of His presence, and a soul that is always reaching out to Him in love and trust. When we live this way, calling on God becomes as natural as breathing, and we begin to experience the peace and joy that come from knowing that we are never alone, that God is always with us, and that we can turn to Him in every moment of our lives.

One of the most powerful things about calling on God is that it invites His presence into our circumstances. When we call on God, we are not just asking for His help; we are inviting Him to step into our situation and to work in ways that only He can. We are acknowledging that we need His power, His wisdom, and His grace to navigate the challenges we are facing. And when God steps in, everything changes. He brings peace to the storm, comfort to the brokenhearted, strength to the weary, and hope to the hopeless. When we call on God, we are opening the door for Him to work in our lives, to bring healing, restoration, and transformation. His presence brings light to the darkest places, hope to the most desperate situations, and life to the places that feel dead. There is no situation too difficult for God, no problem too complex, and no burden too heavy. When we call on Him, He moves in ways that are beyond our comprehension, bringing about solutions, answers, and miracles that we never could have imagined.

Calling on God also teaches us patience and trust in His timing. Sometimes when we call on God, His answer doesn't come right away, or it doesn't come in the way we expect. But even in the waiting, God is working. He is teaching us to trust Him, to rely on His timing, and to believe that He knows what is best for us. Calling on God is an act of faith that says, "God, I trust You, even when I don't see the answer yet. I believe that You are working, even when I don't understand." This kind of trust deepens our relationship with God, because it teaches us to depend on Him not just for the outcome, but for the journey. It teaches us to rest in His faithfulness, knowing that He is always good and that He will never leave us or forsake us.

As you continue through "Answer the Call – 31 Days of Bold Biblical Action", let this call to "Call unto me" be an invitation to deepen your relationship with God through prayer. If there are areas of your life where you have been carrying burdens on your own, or if there are questions and fears that have been weighing you down, now is the time to call on God. He is inviting you to bring everything to Him, to trust Him with the things that are too heavy for you to carry, and to believe that He will answer you. You don't have to have all the answers—you just have to call on the One who does. You don't have to carry your burdens alone—God is inviting you to cast them on Him and to trust that He will take care of you.

Call unto God, and experience the peace, the comfort, and the strength that come from knowing that He hears you and that He will answer you. Call on Him in the quiet moments, in the busy moments, in the moments of joy, and in the moments of pain. Call on Him, and let Him meet you right where you are, bringing His love, His grace, and His presence into every part of your life. Call unto Him, and watch as He works in ways that go beyond what you could ever ask or imagine. Call on Him, and know that He is faithful, that He cares for you, and that He will answer you in His perfect timing and in His perfect way. Call unto the Lord, and rest in the assurance that He is with you, that He hears you, and that He will never let you go.

Chapter 20 – Wait

In the twentieth call to action from "Answer the Call – 31 Days of Bold Biblical Action", we find one of the most challenging yet profoundly rewarding commands from God: "Wait on the LORD: be of good courage, and he shall strengthen thine heart: wait, I say, on the LORD." (Psalm 27:14). These words seem so simple, yet they carry a weight of meaning that speaks to the very heart of our human experience. Waiting is not something that comes naturally to us. In a world that moves at breakneck speed, where instant gratification is the norm, and where waiting often feels like wasted time, the call to "wait on the Lord" can feel like a heavy burden. But it is in this waiting that some of the deepest and most beautiful work of God happens in our lives. To wait on the Lord is not a passive act of standing still, but an active, intentional posture of faith and trust. It means trusting God's timing, trusting His plan, and trusting His heart, even when we don't see the answers we long for. It's about choosing to believe that God is working, even when we can't see it, and that His timing is always perfect, even when it feels delayed.

To wait on the Lord means to place our hope in Him, to lean into His promises, and to rest in the knowledge that He is faithful. It's about holding onto the truth that God knows what is best for us, that He is in control, and that His ways are higher than our ways. Waiting on the Lord requires courage because it means letting go of our need for immediate answers, our desire to control the outcome, and our impatience with the process. It means surrendering our timeline to God's timeline and trusting that His plans for us are good, even when the waiting feels long and difficult. The call to "be of good courage" reminds us that waiting is not for the faint of heart. It takes strength to wait, especially when life feels uncertain, when our prayers seem unanswered, and when the future is unclear. But it is in these moments of waiting that our faith is tested and refined, where we learn to rely on God in ways that we never would if everything came easily or quickly.

Waiting on the Lord often means waiting in the silence. There are times in our lives when God seems quiet, when we are crying out for direction, for breakthrough, or for a miracle, and the heavens seem still. In these moments, it can be tempting to think that God has forgotten us or that He is not listening. But the truth is, God is always at work, even in the silence. He is working behind the scenes, preparing things in ways that we cannot see, shaping us, and drawing us closer to Himself. Waiting on the Lord teaches us to trust in His presence, even when we cannot hear His voice as clearly as we would like. It teaches us to have faith in His promises, even when the fulfillment seems far off. In the silence, God is building in us the kind of deep, unshakable trust that comes from knowing that He is faithful, even when we don't understand His ways.

Waiting on the Lord also involves learning patience. Patience is a fruit of the Spirit, but it is one that often grows in the soil of waiting. In our fast-paced world, where everything is available at the click of a button, patience can feel like a lost art. But when we wait on the Lord, we are learning to cultivate patience—the ability to trust God's process, to endure with grace, and to remain steadfast even when the waiting feels long. Patience is not passive resignation; it is active trust. It is choosing to stay hopeful, to keep praying, to keep believing, and to keep trusting, even when we don't see immediate results. Patience is what enables us to wait well, to wait with expectation rather than frustration, and to trust that God's timing is always right.

Waiting on the Lord is often a time of preparation. There are seasons in our lives when we are waiting for a breakthrough, for an answer to prayer, for a new opportunity, or for God to move in a specific way. But in these seasons of waiting, God is often preparing us for what is to come. He is shaping our character, deepening our faith, and growing our trust in Him. Just as a farmer plants seeds and waits for them to grow, knowing that the growth takes time, God is planting seeds in our hearts during the waiting season, and He is cultivating something beautiful within us. Waiting is not wasted time—it is time of preparation, where God is doing a work in us that we may not fully understand until later. He is preparing us for the blessings, the responsibilities, and the opportunities that are ahead, and sometimes the waiting is necessary to get us ready for what He has in store.

One of the hardest parts of waiting on the Lord is the uncertainty that often comes with it. When we are waiting, we don't always know how things will turn out. We don't know when the answer will come, when the door will open, or when the situation will change. This uncertainty can lead to anxiety, fear, and doubt. But it is in the midst of this uncertainty that God invites us to lean into Him more deeply. Waiting on the Lord requires us to let go of our need for control and to trust that God is in control. It teaches us to surrender our plans, our fears, and our doubts to Him, and to trust that He is working all things together for our good (Romans 8:28). In the uncertainty, God is inviting us to draw closer to Him, to seek His face, and to find our peace in His presence.

Waiting on the Lord is also an opportunity to grow in faith. Faith is believing in what we cannot see, trusting in what we do not yet have, and holding onto the promises of God, even when they seem distant. When we wait on the Lord, we are exercising our faith. We are choosing to believe that God is good, that He is faithful, and that He will fulfill His promises, even when the fulfillment seems far off. Waiting stretches our faith because it forces us to trust in God's timing rather than our own. It reminds us that God's ways are higher than our ways and that His thoughts are higher than our thoughts (Isaiah 55:9). Waiting on the Lord is a faith-building exercise, where we learn to trust Him more deeply, to rely on His Word, and to believe that He is working even when we cannot see it.

In the waiting, God often does some of His deepest work in our hearts. He uses the waiting season to refine us, to strip away the things that are hindering our growth, and to draw us closer to Himself. Waiting reveals what is in our hearts—it exposes our fears, our doubts, and our impatience. But it is in this place of vulnerability that God meets us with His grace. He comforts us, strengthens us, and reassures us of His love. Waiting on the Lord teaches us to depend on Him in ways that we never would if everything came easily. It is in the waiting that we experience the sufficiency of His grace, the depth of His love, and the power of His presence. Waiting on the Lord is not just about waiting for an answer—it's about waiting with Him, allowing Him to be our strength, our peace, and our hope in the midst of uncertainty.

The call to "be of good courage" in Psalm 27:14 reminds us that waiting is not for the faint of heart. It takes courage to wait on the Lord, especially when the waiting is long and difficult. But the courage we are called to is not a self-generated strength—it is a courage that comes from knowing who God is and trusting in His faithfulness. It is the courage to keep believing when the situation looks hopeless, to keep praying when the answers don't come, and to keep trusting when we don't understand. It is the courage to wait with expectation, knowing that God is faithful and that He will come through in His perfect timing. This courage is rooted in the character of God—His goodness, His faithfulness, and His love. When we know who God is, we can wait with courage, because we know that He will not fail us.

Waiting on the Lord is not easy, but it is worth it. Throughout Scripture, we see the stories of men and women who waited on the Lord—Abraham and Sarah waiting for the promised child, Joseph waiting for the fulfillment of his dreams, David waiting to become king, and the Israelites waiting for deliverance. In each of these stories, God was faithful. He fulfilled His promises in His perfect timing, and the waiting was not in vain. Their waiting was a time of preparation, growth, and deepening trust in God. And just as God was faithful to them, He will be faithful to us. When we wait on the Lord, we can trust that He is working, that He has a plan, and that He will fulfill His promises in His perfect timing.

As you continue through "Answer the Call – 31 Days of Bold Biblical Action", let this call to "wait on the Lord" be an invitation to trust in His timing, His plan, and His faithfulness. If you are in a season of waiting—whether you are waiting for an answer to prayer, for direction, for healing, or for breakthrough—know that God sees you, He hears you, and He is with you in the waiting. Waiting is not a sign that God has forgotten you; it is an opportunity for you to draw closer to Him, to grow in faith, and to experience His presence in a deeper way.

Wait on the Lord, and be of good courage, knowing that He is working all things together for your good. Wait on the Lord, and trust that His timing is perfect, even when it feels delayed. Wait on the Lord, and find strength in His presence, peace in His promises, and hope in His faithfulness. Wait on the Lord, and know that He is with you, that He loves you, and that He will never leave you or forsake you. Waiting is not easy, but it is an opportunity to experience the depth of God's love and faithfulness in ways that we could never imagine.

Wait on the Lord, and watch as He works in your heart, in your life, and in your circumstances. Wait on the Lord, and be of good courage, for He is faithful, and He will fulfill His promises in His perfect timing.

Chapter 21 – Hear

In the twenty-first call to action from "Answer the Call – 31 Days of Bold Biblical Action", we are confronted with one of the most profound challenges from Jesus Himself: "He that hath ears to hear, let him hear." (Matthew 11:15). This simple yet deeply powerful command goes beyond the physical act of hearing—it calls us to truly listen, to open our hearts and minds to the voice of God, and to be transformed by what we hear. Jesus often used this phrase after sharing parables or teachings that carried deep spiritual truths, urging His listeners to not just hear the words but to understand, to absorb, and to apply them to their lives. Hearing, in this sense, is an act of spiritual openness, a willingness to be changed by the truth of God's Word. It's about being attentive to His voice, recognizing His truth, and responding in obedience. To "hear" in the way Jesus speaks of is to tune out the noise of the world and to tune into the voice of the Holy Spirit, who speaks to us through Scripture, through prayer, and through the quiet moments of our lives. It is an invitation to go deeper, to move beyond surface-level understanding, and to allow God's Word to penetrate our hearts and shape the way we live.

In a world filled with distractions and constant noise, the ability to truly hear is more important than ever. We live in a time where information is everywhere, but wisdom can be scarce. We are bombarded by voices—from media, culture, social circles, and our own internal thoughts—all vying for our attention, pulling us in different directions, and often drowning out the voice of God. When Jesus says, "He that hath ears to hear, let him hear," He is calling us to be intentional about how we listen, to seek His voice above all others, and to quiet the noise around us so that we can hear what He is saying to us. This kind of hearing requires more than just passive listening; it demands active engagement, a heart that is ready and willing to receive what God is speaking, and a life that is ready to be shaped by His truth. It's about creating space in our lives to hear from God, to meditate on His Word, and to be open to the ways He is leading us, even when it challenges us or calls us to change.

To truly hear means to listen with humility. It requires us to admit that we don't have all the answers, that we need God's wisdom and guidance, and that we are willing to be taught. Hearing in the biblical sense is about being teachable, about having a heart that is open to correction, instruction, and growth. When we come before God with ears to hear, we are saying, "Lord, I am ready to listen to You. I am ready to be changed by Your Word, to align my life with Your truth, and to follow where You lead." This kind of humility is essential if we are going to grow in our faith and walk in obedience to God's calling. It's about setting aside our own opinions, preferences, and desires, and allowing God's Word to shape our thinking and our actions.

But hearing God's voice is not always easy. There are times when God speaks in ways that we may not expect—through a quiet whisper, through a passage of Scripture that convicts us, through the wise counsel of a friend, or through the circumstances of our lives. Sometimes His voice may challenge us, calling us to step out in faith, to let go of something we've been holding onto, or to make a difficult decision. Other times, His voice may bring comfort, peace, and reassurance in the midst of trials or uncertainty. But no matter how God speaks, we must be willing to listen, to trust that His voice is always for our good, and to obey what He is calling us to do. Hearing from God is not just about gaining knowledge; it's about responding in faith and obedience to what He reveals to us.

One of the most important aspects of hearing is discernment. In a world where so many voices compete for our attention, we need to be able to discern which voices are from God and which are not. The enemy often tries to sow confusion, doubt, and fear, whispering lies that can lead us astray if we are not grounded in God's truth. This is why it is so important to spend time in God's Word, to know His voice, and to align our lives with His truth. Jesus said that His sheep know His voice and follow Him (John 10:27). This means that as we grow in our relationship with God, we will become more attuned to His voice, more sensitive to the leading of the Holy Spirit, and more able to discern His truth from the lies of the enemy. Discernment is not something that happens overnight—it is developed through time spent with God, through prayer, and through a deepening relationship with Him.

Hearing from God is also about being sensitive to the prompting of the Holy Spirit in our daily lives. Sometimes God speaks in unexpected ways—through a nudge in our spirit, a sense of peace, or a conviction that we cannot shake. These moments of prompting are often God's way of guiding us, leading us to take action, or drawing our attention to something important. But we must be listening, we must have ears to hear, if we are going to recognize these moments and respond in obedience. Too often, we miss what God is saying because we are too busy, too distracted, or too caught up in our own plans. But when we cultivate a posture of listening—when we slow down, create space for God, and invite Him to speak—we open ourselves up to the incredible ways He wants to lead and direct our lives.

Hearing from God is not just about hearing for ourselves; it's also about hearing for others. As followers of Christ, we are called to be a light to the world, to share the love of God with those around us, and to speak His truth into the lives of others. But in order to do this effectively, we must first be able to hear from God ourselves. We cannot give what we have not received. When we hear from God, we are filled with His wisdom, His love, and His truth, and we are then able to pour that out into the lives of others. Whether it's offering a word of encouragement, sharing a scripture that God has placed on our hearts, or simply being a listening ear to someone in need, hearing from God equips us to be His hands and feet in the world.

Jesus' call to "hear" is also a call to action. Hearing is not complete until it leads to obedience. Throughout Scripture, we see that when God speaks, He often calls His people to respond in some way—to step out in faith, to trust Him, to obey His commands, or to take a specific action. When we hear from God, it is not enough to simply listen and do nothing; we are called to respond in faith, to act on what He has revealed to us, and to live out His truth in our daily lives. James 1:22 reminds us to be doers of the Word, not just hearers. Hearing is the first step, but it must lead to action if we are going to walk in obedience to God's will. When we hear from God and respond in faith, we position ourselves to experience His blessings, His guidance, and His presence in new and powerful ways.

But hearing from God requires intentionality. It requires us to create space in our lives to listen, to seek Him, and to be still in His presence. In our busy, noisy world, it is easy to rush through life without ever stopping to listen to what God is saying. But if we want to hear from Him, we must make time for Him. We must carve out moments of quiet, where we can open His Word, pray, and listen for His voice. We must be willing to turn off the distractions, to silence the noise, and to focus on Him. God is always speaking, but we must be willing to listen. When we prioritize time with God, when we seek Him with all our hearts, we will find Him (Jeremiah 29:13), and we will hear His voice more clearly.

Hearing from God also requires a heart that is surrendered to Him. It is possible to hear God's voice and yet choose to ignore it, to resist what He is calling us to do, or to harden our hearts against His leading. But true hearing is about surrender—it's about saying, "Lord, I am listening, and I am willing to follow wherever You lead." It's about trusting that God's plans for us are good, even when they are different from our own, and being willing to let go of our own agendas in order to follow His will. When we come before God with a surrendered heart, ready to listen and obey, we position ourselves to receive all that He has for us.

As you continue through "Answer the Call – 31 Days of Bold Biblical Action", let this call to "hear" be an invitation to open your ears, your heart, and your life to the voice of God. If there are areas of your life where you have been too busy, too distracted, or too resistant to hear from Him, now is the time to quiet the noise, to seek Him, and to listen for His voice. God is speaking—through His Word, through His Spirit, and through the circumstances of your life. He is calling you to hear, to receive His truth, and to respond in faith.

He that hath ears to hear, let him hear. Let this be the moment when you choose to listen deeply to what God is saying to you, to open your heart to His leading, and to trust that His voice is leading you in the way you should go. Hear His voice, and allow it to shape your life, your decisions, and your future. Hear, and respond in faith, knowing that God's voice is always speaking for your good, to lead you into deeper relationship with Him and to guide you into the fullness of life He has for you. Hear, and be transformed by the power of His Word, by the depth of His love, and by the truth of His promises.

He that hath ears to hear, let him hear, and experience the joy, peace, and fulfillment that come from living in tune with the voice of God.

Chapter 22 – Confess

In the twenty-second call to action from "Answer the Call – 31 Days of Bold Biblical Action", we are invited into one of the most powerful and transformative promises in Scripture: "If we confess our sins, he is faithful and just to forgive us our sins, and to cleanse us from all unrighteousness." (1 John 1:9). These words carry the weight of the gospel message, offering hope, healing, and freedom to anyone burdened by the guilt, shame, or weight of their sin. Confession is the key that unlocks the door to God's forgiveness, grace, and redemption. It is an act of vulnerability and humility, where we come before God, acknowledging our brokenness, admitting our wrongs, and laying down the weight of our mistakes. Confession is not about condemnation—it is about liberation. It is about stepping into the light of God's truth, letting go of the things that keep us from Him, and allowing His grace to wash over us, cleansing us from all unrighteousness. To confess our sins is to acknowledge that we have fallen short, that we have missed the mark, but it is also to acknowledge that God, in His love and mercy, is ready and willing to forgive us completely.

Confession requires honesty—not just with God, but with ourselves. It asks us to take an honest look at our hearts and admit the areas where we have turned away from God's ways, where we have chosen selfishness over love, pride over humility, or fear over faith. Confession is an act of surrender, where we stop pretending, stop justifying, and stop hiding. It is the moment when we say, "Lord, I have sinned. I have strayed from Your path. I need Your forgiveness." But confession is not about wallowing in guilt; it is about freedom. God doesn't ask us to confess so that we will feel condemned—He asks us to confess so that we can be free from the chains of sin and guilt that weigh us down. His desire is not to punish us but to restore us, to reconcile us to Himself, and to renew our hearts. When we confess our sins, we are not met with judgment; we are met with grace.

One of the most beautiful aspects of this promise is the assurance of God's faithfulness. "He is faithful and just to forgive." This means that God's forgiveness is not dependent on our worthiness, our efforts, or our ability to fix ourselves. It is dependent on His character. God is faithful—He never changes, He never goes back on His Word, and He never withholds His forgiveness from those who seek it with a sincere heart. When we confess our sins, we can be confident that God will forgive us, not because we deserve it, but because He is faithful to His promise. He is just, meaning that His forgiveness is rooted in His righteousness. He forgives us not because He overlooks our sin, but because Jesus has already paid the price for our sin on the cross. Our confession is the means by which we receive the forgiveness that has already been won for us through Jesus' sacrifice. In confessing, we are claiming the gift of grace that God has freely given to us.

Confession also brings healing. James 5:16 tells us to "confess your sins to one another and pray for one another, that you may be healed." There is something profoundly healing about bringing our sins into the light, both before God and before trusted brothers and sisters in Christ. When we keep our sins hidden, they fester in the dark, growing heavier and more burdensome. But when we confess them, we release the power they have over us. We allow God's light to shine into the darkest parts of our hearts, and in that light, we find healing. Confession breaks the chains of shame that often keep us bound, and it opens the door for God's grace to bring healing and restoration. It also strengthens our relationships with others, as it fosters an environment of honesty, vulnerability, and mutual support.

Confession is not just about admitting the things we have done wrong; it is also about turning away from those things. True confession is accompanied by repentance, which means a change of heart, a turning away from sin, and a turning back to God. When we confess our sins, we are not simply saying, "I'm sorry"—we are committing to walk in a new direction, to live in a way that aligns with God's will and His ways. This is why confession is so transformative—it is not just about receiving forgiveness for the past, but about stepping into a new future, one that is marked by God's grace and guided by His truth. Repentance is a daily practice, a continual turning back to God, and confession is the first step in that process. It is the moment when we lay down the weight of our sins and receive the strength to walk in a new way.

But confession also requires courage. It takes courage to admit that we have messed up, that we have hurt others, or that we have failed to live up to God's standards. It takes courage to be vulnerable before God, to admit that we are broken and in need of His healing. But the courage to confess is met with the overwhelming grace of God, who is always ready to forgive. God does not want us to be afraid of coming to Him with our sins. He knows our weaknesses, and His heart is full of compassion for us. The Bible tells us that God is "slow to anger and abounding in steadfast love" (Psalm 103:8). He is not waiting to condemn us—He is waiting to welcome us with open arms, to forgive us, and to restore us to right relationship with Him. When we confess, we are not approaching a harsh judge, but a loving Father who is eager to forgive and to set us free.

Confession is also a way of growing in our relationship with God. Just as in any relationship, honesty is key to intimacy. When we confess our sins, we are being honest with God, and that honesty deepens our relationship with Him. It allows us to experience His love in a deeper way, because we realize that even in our brokenness, even in our sin, God still loves us. His love is not based on our performance or our ability to get everything right—it is based on who He is, and He is love. When we confess, we are reminded of His unconditional love, His grace, and His mercy. And in that reminder, we find the strength to continue walking with Him, trusting that His grace is sufficient for us in every moment.

Moreover, confession keeps our hearts soft toward God. When we fail to confess, our hearts can become hardened by sin. We can begin to justify our actions, to make excuses, or to ignore the conviction of the Holy Spirit. But when we confess regularly, we keep our hearts open and sensitive to God's voice. We allow Him to continually shape us, mold us, and guide us in the way we should go. Confession keeps us humble, reminding us that we are not perfect, but we are perfectly loved by a God who is committed to transforming us into the image of His Son. It keeps us dependent on His grace, knowing that we cannot walk this journey of faith on our own, but that we need His strength, His guidance, and His forgiveness every day.

Confession is also an invitation to freedom. So many people walk around carrying the weight of guilt and shame, believing that they are defined by their mistakes, their failures, or their past. But God offers us a way out of that burden—He offers us forgiveness, freedom, and a fresh start. When we confess our sins, we are not just letting go of the past; we are stepping into the freedom that Christ has won for us. We are no longer defined by our sins—we are defined by God's grace. We are no longer bound by guilt or shame—we are set free by the love of God. This is the power of confession: it breaks the chains of sin and allows us to live in the freedom and joy that come from being forgiven.

As you continue through "Answer the Call – 31 Days of Bold Biblical Action", let this call to "confess" be an invitation to experience the freedom, healing, and grace that come from bringing your sins before God. If there are areas of your life where you have been holding onto guilt, shame, or unconfessed sin, now is the time to bring them into the light. God is faithful and just—He is ready and willing to forgive you, to cleanse you, and to restore you. Don't let the weight of your past hold you back any longer. Confess your sins to God, and receive the forgiveness that He offers through Jesus Christ.

Confess, and experience the healing that comes from being honest with God, from laying down your burdens, and from stepping into the light of His grace. Confess, and allow God's love to wash over you, cleansing you from all unrighteousness and filling you with His peace. Confess, and be reminded that you are not defined by your mistakes—you are defined by God's grace. Confess, and walk in the freedom that comes from knowing that you are forgiven, that you are loved, and that you are a new creation in Christ.

Confess, and be of good courage, knowing that God is faithful and just to forgive you, to cleanse you, and to make all things new in your life. Confess, and step into the fullness of life that God has for you—a life marked by His grace, His forgiveness, and His love. Confess, and know that there is no sin too great for God's forgiveness, no mistake too big for His grace, and no burden too heavy for His love. Confess, and be set free.

Chapter 23 – Abide

In the twenty-third call to action from "Answer the Call – 31 Days of Bold Biblical Action", we encounter one of the most profound and intimate invitations from Jesus: "Abide in me, and I in you. As the branch cannot bear fruit of itself, except it abide in the vine; no more can ye, except ye abide in me." (John 15:4). These words are not just a command but a deeply personal invitation into a life-transforming relationship with Christ. To "abide" means to remain, to dwell, to stay connected, and to live in a continual, unbroken communion with Jesus. It's not just about being near Jesus—it's about being rooted in Him, drawing your life, strength, and purpose from Him in every moment of every day. Jesus is inviting us to experience a relationship that is not based on occasional encounters or fleeting emotions but on a constant, daily, abiding presence with Him. This call to abide in Jesus is at the very heart of what it means to be a follower of Christ. It is an invitation to make Jesus the center of our lives, the source of our identity, our joy, and our strength. It is a call to live in such close relationship with Him that His life flows through us, like the life-giving sap that flows through a vine and its branches, nourishing them and enabling them to bear fruit.

To abide in Christ means that we are not living for ourselves, but we are living in deep, intimate fellowship with Him. It means that our lives are no longer driven by our own desires, ambitions, or fears, but by His love, His will, and His presence. Abiding in Christ is not about striving or working harder to earn God's favor—it is about resting in His love, trusting in His grace, and allowing Him to work in and through us. It is a life of surrender, where we let go of our need for control and allow Jesus to be the Lord of every part of our lives. When we abide in Christ, we are no longer living in our own strength, but in the power of His Spirit. His presence fills us, His peace sustains us, and His joy becomes our strength. Abiding in Christ is not just a spiritual concept—it is a way of life, where every moment is lived in the awareness of His presence and every decision is guided by His wisdom.

Jesus uses the metaphor of the vine and branches in John 15 to describe this relationship of abiding. He is the vine, and we are the branches. Just as a branch cannot survive or bear fruit unless it is connected to the vine, we cannot truly live or bear fruit unless we are connected to Jesus. When we are disconnected from Him, we wither. Our spiritual life dries up, and we become like a branch that is cut off from its source of life. But when we abide in Him, we are nourished, we grow, and we bear fruit. This fruit is not just about doing good works—it is about the fruit of the Spirit growing in us: love, joy, peace, patience, kindness, goodness, faithfulness, gentleness, and self-control (Galatians 5:22-23). This fruit is the evidence of Christ's life flowing through us. It is not something we can produce on our own—it is the natural result of abiding in Him.

Abiding in Christ also means staying connected to His Word. Jesus said, "If you abide in me, and my words abide in you, ask whatever you wish, and it will be done for you" (John 15:7). To abide in Jesus is to let His words shape our thoughts, guide our actions, and transform our hearts. It means that we don't just read the Bible occasionally, but we meditate on it, allow it to dwell in us, and let it become the foundation of our lives. When we let God's Word abide in us, it changes us from the inside out. It renews our minds, gives us wisdom, and strengthens our faith. It helps us to see the world through God's eyes, to align our desires with His, and to live according to His truth. Abiding in Christ is about staying rooted in His Word, letting it dwell in us richly, and allowing it to bear fruit in our lives.

One of the most beautiful aspects of abiding in Christ is the promise that He will abide in us. Jesus says, "Abide in me, and I in you." This is not a one-sided relationship. When we choose to abide in Jesus, He abides in us. His presence is not distant or far off—it is personal, intimate, and constant. He promises to dwell in our hearts through faith (Ephesians 3:17), to be with us always (Matthew 28:20), and to never leave us or forsake us (Hebrews 13:5). When we abide in Christ, we are never alone. His presence is with us in every moment, guiding us, comforting us, and giving us strength. Abiding in Christ is about experiencing the reality of His presence in our daily lives, knowing that He is closer than our next breath and that His love is constant and unchanging.

Abiding in Christ also brings peace. In a world filled with chaos, uncertainty, and fear, abiding in Jesus is the source of true peace. Jesus said, "Peace I leave with you; my peace I give to you" (John 14:27). This peace is not dependent on our circumstances—it comes from knowing that we are held in the hands of a loving and sovereign God. When we abide in Christ, we experience a peace that surpasses all understanding (Philippians 4:7). It is a peace that comes from trusting that God is in control, that He is working all things together for our good (Romans 8:28), and that nothing can separate us from His love (Romans 8:38-39). Abiding in Christ allows us to rest in His peace, even in the midst of trials, because we know that He is with us and that His grace is sufficient for us in every situation.

But abiding in Christ is not always easy. There are times when the pressures of life, the distractions of the world, or the struggles we face can pull us away from our connection with Jesus. In these moments, it can be tempting to rely on our own strength, to try to fix things on our own, or to let worry and fear take over. But Jesus invites us to return to Him, to stay connected to Him, and to let Him carry our burdens. Abiding in Christ means choosing to remain in Him, even when it's difficult, even when we don't feel like it, and even when the circumstances of life are overwhelming. It means trusting that He is enough, that His grace is sufficient, and that His presence is what we need most. Abiding in Christ is a choice we make every day—to stay connected to Him, to rely on Him, and to let His life flow through us.

Abiding in Christ also requires dependence. Just as a branch depends on the vine for its life and growth, we must depend on Jesus for everything. He is the source of our strength, our wisdom, and our ability to bear fruit. When we abide in Him, we are acknowledging our dependence on Him, recognizing that apart from Him, we can do nothing (John 15:5). This dependence is not a sign of weakness—it is a sign of trust. It is an acknowledgment that we are not self-sufficient, that we need Jesus in every aspect of our lives, and that we are willing to rely on His grace, His power, and His provision. Abiding in Christ means letting go of our pride, our self-reliance, and our need for control, and trusting that He will provide for us, guide us, and work in and through us in ways that we could never accomplish on our own.

One of the most important aspects of abiding in Christ is the intimacy it brings. Abiding is about being with Jesus, not just doing things for Him. It is about cultivating a relationship with Him, spending time in His presence, and getting to know His heart. When we abide in Christ, we grow in our intimacy with Him. We learn to hear His voice, to recognize His leading, and to experience the depth of His love for us. This intimacy is not something that can be rushed or manufactured—it is the result of spending time with Jesus, of drawing near to Him, and of allowing Him to draw near to us. It is about sitting at His feet, listening to His voice, and letting His love fill our hearts. Abiding in Christ is about making Him the priority of our lives, the center of our attention, and the focus of our love.

As you continue through "Answer the Call – 31 Days of Bold Biblical Action", let this call to "abide" be an invitation to deepen your relationship with Jesus, to remain in His presence, and to experience the fullness of life that comes from being connected to Him. If there are areas of your life where you have been trying to go it alone, where you have been disconnected from Jesus, now is the time to return to Him. He is inviting you to abide in Him, to rest in His love, and to let His life flow through you. Abide in Jesus, and experience the peace, the joy, and the strength that come from being rooted in Him.

Abide in Him, and let His Word dwell in you richly. Abide in Him, and let His presence guide you in every decision, every conversation, and every moment of your day. Abide in Him, and trust that He is working in you and through you to bear fruit for His kingdom. Abide in Him, and know that you are never alone—He is with you, He is for you, and His love for you is unchanging.

Abide in Jesus, and watch as your life becomes a reflection of His love, His grace, and His truth. Abide in Him, and experience the transformation that comes from living in constant communion with the Savior of the world. Abide in Him, and let His life flow through you, bearing fruit that will last for eternity. Abide in Him, and rest in the assurance that His presence is enough, His grace is sufficient, and His love for you is everlasting.

Abide in me, and I in you. Let these words be the foundation of your life, the source of your strength, and the joy of your heart. Abide in Jesus, and experience the fullness of life that only comes from being connected to the true Vine.

Chapter 24 – Bless

In the twenty-fourth call to action from "Answer the Call – 31 Days of Bold Biblical Action", we are confronted with one of the most challenging and radical commands Jesus ever gave: "Bless them that curse you, and pray for them which despitefully use you." (Luke 6:28). This command goes against every instinct of our human nature. When we are hurt, mistreated, or cursed by others, our natural reaction is to defend ourselves, seek revenge, or respond with anger. But Jesus calls us to a higher way of living, one that reflects the radical love and grace of God. To "bless" someone who curses you means to speak well of them, to pray for their good, and to desire God's blessings over their life, even when they have hurt you. This kind of response is not natural—it is supernatural. It is the kind of love that only comes from a heart transformed by the love of Christ. Jesus is calling us to step out of the cycle of hurt and retaliation and into the freedom that comes from loving others as He has loved us. It is a call to break the chains of bitterness, anger, and unforgiveness, and to extend grace, mercy, and kindness to even our worst enemies.

When Jesus tells us to bless those who curse us, He is inviting us to reflect His own heart. On the cross, Jesus prayed for those who were crucifying Him, saying, "Father, forgive them, for they know not what they do" (Luke 23:34). He did not respond to their cruelty with hatred or revenge—He responded with love, mercy, and forgiveness. In the same way, Jesus is calling us to respond to those who hurt us with love and grace. This does not mean that we ignore the pain or pretend that the hurt never happened, but it does mean that we choose to let go of our desire for revenge and instead trust God to bring healing and justice in His time and in His way. To bless those who curse us means that we refuse to let their actions dictate our response. Instead of responding with bitterness, we choose to respond with love. Instead of cursing them in return, we pray for them. Instead of holding onto anger, we release them into God's hands and ask Him to work in their hearts.

Blessing those who curse us is one of the most powerful ways we can demonstrate the love of Christ to the world. It is a love that is not based on what others deserve but on the grace that God has shown us. The truth is, we were once enemies of God, separated from Him by our sin. Yet, in His incredible love, He reached out to us, blessed us, and offered us forgiveness through Jesus Christ. When we bless those who curse us, we are reflecting the heart of God, who loves His enemies and desires that all people come to repentance and salvation. This kind of love is shocking to the world because it is so different from the way the world operates. The world teaches us to seek revenge, to hold grudges, and to give people what they deserve. But Jesus teaches us to love our enemies, to pray for those who persecute us, and to bless those who curse us. This kind of love is not weak—it is the most powerful force in the world because it has the power to change hearts, heal wounds, and bring people to the knowledge of God's love.

Blessing those who curse us is also about freedom. When we hold onto anger, bitterness, or unforgiveness, we are the ones who are bound. These negative emotions can consume us, robbing us of peace, joy, and even physical health. But when we choose to bless those who have hurt us, we are setting ourselves free from the chains of bitterness and anger. We are choosing to live in the freedom that Christ has given us, where our hearts are not weighed down by the offenses of others, but are filled with His love and grace. Blessing those who curse us does not mean that we condone their actions or that we allow ourselves to be mistreated—it means that we choose to respond in a way that reflects the love of Christ, trusting that He will bring justice and healing. It is an act of faith, where we trust God to handle the situation and to work in the hearts of those who have wronged us.

One of the most challenging aspects of this command is that it requires us to surrender our desire for control. When we are hurt, we often want to control the situation, to make sure that the person who hurt us gets what they deserve. But Jesus calls us to let go of that desire for control and to trust Him to bring justice in His time and in His way. This requires humility, because it means acknowledging that we don't have all the answers and that we don't always know what is best. It requires us to trust that God sees the bigger picture, that He knows what is in the hearts of those who have hurt us, and that He will bring about the right outcome. When we bless those who curse us, we are choosing to trust that God is the ultimate judge, and that His justice is perfect.

Blessing those who curse us is also a way of protecting our hearts. When we hold onto anger and bitterness, it can harden our hearts, making it difficult for us to experience the fullness of God's love and grace. But when we choose to bless others, even those who have hurt us, we are keeping our hearts soft and open to God's love. We are allowing His grace to flow through us, and in doing so, we are protecting our hearts from becoming hardened by the pain we have experienced. This is not easy—it requires us to constantly come before God in prayer, asking Him to help us forgive, to help us love, and to help us bless those who have wronged us. But as we do, we find that our hearts become more like His—filled with love, grace, and compassion.

Blessing those who curse us is also an act of spiritual warfare. The enemy wants to keep us trapped in anger, bitterness, and unforgiveness because he knows that these things will keep us from experiencing the fullness of God's love and power. But when we choose to bless those who curse us, we are breaking the enemy's hold over our lives. We are refusing to let bitterness and anger take root in our hearts, and instead, we are choosing to live in the freedom and love that Christ has given us. This is one of the ways that we overcome evil with good (Romans 12:21). When we bless those who curse us, we are declaring that the love of Christ is more powerful than the hate, hurt, or anger that others may direct toward us.

This command to "bless them that curse you" also reminds us of the power of prayer. One of the most practical ways we can bless those who curse us is by praying for them. When we pray for those who have hurt us, we are asking God to work in their hearts, to bring healing, and to lead them to repentance. Prayer is a powerful weapon because it invites God to intervene in situations where we feel powerless. When we pray for our enemies, we are aligning our hearts with God's heart, asking Him to bring about His will in their lives. Prayer is also a way of releasing our anger and hurt into God's hands, trusting Him to bring about healing and restoration. As we pray for those who have hurt us, we may find that our own hearts begin to soften, and that we are able to see them through God's eyes—people who are in need of His love and grace, just as we are.

Blessing those who curse us is not something we can do in our own strength. It requires the power of the Holy Spirit working in us to love others in the way that Jesus has loved us. We cannot muster up this kind of love on our own—it comes from abiding in Christ, being filled with His love, and allowing His Spirit to transform our hearts. When we are connected to Jesus, His love flows through us, enabling us to love others, even those who have hurt us. This is why it is so important to stay close to Jesus, to spend time in His presence, and to allow His love to fill our hearts. As we abide in Him, we find the strength to bless those who curse us, to love our enemies, and to reflect His love to the world.

As you continue through "Answer the Call – 31 Days of Bold Biblical Action", let this call to "bless them that curse you" be an invitation to live in the radical love and grace of Jesus. If there are people in your life who have hurt you, mistreated you, or cursed you, now is the time to bring those hurts before God and ask Him to help you bless them. This does not mean ignoring the pain or pretending that the hurt never happened, but it does mean choosing to let go of anger and bitterness and to respond with love. Trust that God will bring healing to your heart and that He will work in the lives of those who have wronged you.

Bless those who curse you, and experience the freedom that comes from letting go of anger and bitterness. Bless those who curse you, and watch as God softens your heart, fills you with His love, and strengthens you to love others as He has loved you. Bless those who curse you, and be a witness to the world of the radical love and grace of Jesus Christ. Bless those who curse you, and know that you are reflecting the heart of God, who loves His enemies and who has called you to do the same.

Bless them that curse you, and step into the fullness of the love, grace, and freedom that Christ has given you. Bless them that curse you, and watch as God works in your heart and in the hearts of those who have wronged you, bringing healing, restoration, and peace. Bless them that curse you, and experience the joy that comes from living in the love and grace of Jesus.

Chapter 25 – Behold

In the twenty-fifth call to action from "Answer the Call – 31 Days of Bold Biblical Action", we come face to face with one of the most personal and tender invitations from Jesus: "Behold, I stand at the door, and knock: if any man hear my voice, and open the door, I will come in to him, and will sup with him, and he with me." (Revelation 3:20). These words are filled with love, longing, and urgency as Jesus extends an invitation to each of us, patiently waiting at the door of our hearts. He is not forcing His way in; He is knocking, gently and persistently, offering Himself to us. This is the picture of a Savior who desires a relationship with us, not from a distance, but up close and personal. The word "behold" means to stop and pay attention. Jesus is calling us to pause, to listen, and to recognize that He is standing right outside the door of our hearts, ready to come in if we will only let Him. He isn't distant or detached—He is right here, near, waiting for us to open the door. The image of Jesus standing at the door and knocking is one of the most powerful expressions of His love and desire for intimacy with us. It speaks of a God who pursues us, who doesn't give up on us, and who is always ready to enter into our lives if we will invite Him in.

When Jesus says, "I stand at the door and knock," He is offering us more than just a casual visit. He is offering us His presence, His love, and His peace. He is offering us a relationship that is deep, transformative, and life-giving. But the choice to open the door is ours. Jesus respects our free will—He will not force His way into our hearts. He waits for us to respond to His knock, to hear His voice, and to open the door. This is the beauty of God's love—it is freely given, but it must also be freely received. Jesus is not knocking to condemn us or to demand perfection from us—He is knocking because He wants to be with us. He wants to bring healing to our wounds, peace to our troubled hearts, and joy to our lives. He wants to walk with us through every moment, both the good and the hard, and to be our constant companion. But He will not come in unless we open the door.

The door that Jesus stands at is not just the door to our hearts; it is the door to every part of our lives. For some, the door may be the door of salvation—Jesus is knocking, inviting you to receive Him as your Savior and Lord, to experience the forgiveness and new life that He offers. For others, the door may be the door to a deeper relationship with Him. Perhaps you've known Jesus for a long time, but there are areas of your life where you've kept the door closed, where you haven't fully allowed Him in. Maybe there are fears, doubts, or sins that you've kept hidden behind that door, and Jesus is knocking, gently asking you to let Him in, to bring His light into those dark places, and to bring healing and transformation. Wherever you are in your relationship with Jesus, He is always knocking, always inviting you to go deeper, to open more of your life to Him, and to experience more of His love and presence.

When Jesus knocks at the door, it's not because He needs anything from us—it's because He knows that we need Him. He knows that without Him, our hearts are restless, our souls are empty, and our lives are incomplete. We were created for relationship with God, and until we open the door and invite Him in, there will always be a sense of longing and unfulfilled desire in our hearts. Jesus is the only one who can fill the deepest longings of our souls, the only one who can bring true peace, joy, and purpose to our lives. When we open the door to Jesus, we are inviting Him to be the center of our lives, to lead us, guide us, and transform us. We are saying, "Lord, I need You. I want You in every part of my life." And when we do that, He comes in—He makes His home in our hearts, and we experience the fullness of His love and grace.

The knock of Jesus is persistent but gentle. He doesn't barge in or force His way into our lives. He knocks, and He waits. He waits for us to respond, to recognize our need for Him, and to open the door. His knock is not a demand—it's an invitation. It's an invitation to relationship, to communion, to intimacy. It's an invitation to know Him not just as a distant figure, but as a friend, a Savior, a guide, and a Lord. And the amazing thing is that Jesus doesn't stop knocking. Even when we ignore Him, even when we turn away, even when we're too busy or distracted to hear Him—He keeps knocking. His love is relentless. He pursues us with a love that never gives up, a love that is patient, kind, and unfailing. He will stand at the door and knock for as long as it takes, because He desires to be with us. He desires to enter into every part of our lives and to walk with us in every season.

When we hear the knock of Jesus at the door, we are faced with a choice. We can choose to ignore it, to keep the door closed, or to respond and invite Him in. But we must remember that opening the door is not just a one-time decision—it's a daily choice. Every day, we are faced with the decision to either invite Jesus into our lives or to keep Him at a distance. There will be days when it's easy to open the door—when we feel close to God, when we're experiencing His blessings, and when we're walking in peace. But there will also be days when it's hard—when we're struggling, when we're in pain, when we're doubting, and when we feel far from God. In those moments, Jesus is still knocking. He's still standing at the door, waiting for us to let Him in, to trust Him with our pain, our doubts, and our struggles. And when we open the door, we find that He is faithful. He comes in, He brings peace, and He walks with us through whatever we are facing.

Opening the door to Jesus is an act of faith. It requires us to trust that He is who He says He is, and that He will do what He has promised. It requires us to believe that His presence in our lives is the key to our peace, our joy, and our purpose. It requires us to surrender control, to let go of our fears, and to allow Him to take the lead in our lives. But when we do, we find that Jesus is faithful. He is not a distant God—He is a personal Savior who comes into the very heart of our lives, who knows us intimately, who loves us completely, and who desires to walk with us every step of the way. When we open the door to Jesus, we are opening the door to a life that is full of His presence, His peace, and His love.

Jesus promises that if we open the door, He will come in and dine with us (Revelation 3:20). This image of dining together speaks of fellowship, intimacy, and friendship. In the culture of Jesus' time, sharing a meal with someone was a sign of deep relationship and connection. When Jesus says that He will dine with us, He is offering us the kind of relationship that is not distant or formal, but close, personal, and filled with love. He wants to share life with us—to be a part of our everyday moments, our joys, our struggles, and our dreams. He wants to be the one we turn to for comfort, guidance, and strength. He wants to be the one who fills our hearts with joy and our lives with purpose. When we open the door to Jesus, we are inviting Him into the most intimate parts of our lives, and in return, we experience the fullness of His love and the joy of His presence.

But this invitation to open the door to Jesus is also a call to action. It's not enough to hear the knock—we must respond. We must open the door and invite Him in. This means making space for Him in our lives, prioritizing our relationship with Him, and allowing His Word and His Spirit to shape us. It means surrendering the areas of our lives that we've kept closed off to Him—our fears, our doubts, our sins, and our struggles—and inviting Him to bring His healing and transformation. It means choosing to live each day in fellowship with Him, allowing His presence to guide our decisions, our actions, and our attitudes. When we open the door to Jesus, we are choosing to make Him the center of our lives, and in doing so, we experience the abundant life that He has promised.

As you continue through "Answer the Call – 31 Days of Bold Biblical Action", let this call to "behold" and to open the door to Jesus be an invitation to experience the fullness of His love and presence. If there are areas of your life where you've kept the door closed, now is the time to open it. Jesus is knocking—He is standing at the door of your heart, waiting for you to invite Him in. He is not here to condemn you or to demand perfection—He is here to offer you His love, His grace, and His peace. Open the door to Jesus, and experience the joy of His presence. Open the door, and let Him bring healing to your heart. Open the door, and allow Him to lead you into a deeper relationship with Him.

Behold, He stands at the door and knocks. Let this be the moment when you choose to respond, to open the door, and to invite Him into every part of your life. When you do, you will find that Jesus is faithful. He will come in, He will be with you, and He will never leave you. Behold, He stands at the door—open it, and experience the fullness of His love and the joy of walking in relationship with Him.

Chapter 26 – Take

In the twenty-sixth call to action from "Answer the Call – 31 Days of Bold Biblical Action", we are invited into one of the most comforting and powerful promises from Jesus: "Take my yoke upon you, and learn of me; for I am meek and lowly in heart: and ye shall find rest unto your souls." (Matthew 11:29). These words are not just an invitation—they are an offer of rest, peace, and transformation for weary souls. When Jesus speaks of taking His yoke upon us, He is not offering us a burden that will weigh us down, but rather a partnership with Him that will lighten the load of life's struggles. A yoke in ancient times was a wooden beam used to harness two animals together so they could share the weight of a load, making it easier for both to pull. By using this metaphor, Jesus is offering us a chance to be yoked together with Him, to let Him carry the heavy burdens we've been trying to bear on our own, and to find rest for our souls in the process. It is an invitation to stop striving, to stop trying to do everything in our own strength, and to enter into the freedom and peace that come from walking in step with Jesus, letting Him carry the weight of life's challenges alongside us.

To take Jesus' yoke upon us means that we are surrendering our independence, our self-reliance, and our pride, and choosing instead to walk with Him, to learn from Him, and to follow His lead. It's an invitation to let go of the exhausting pursuit of trying to figure everything out on our own and to trust that Jesus knows the way. His yoke is easy, and His burden is light, not because life suddenly becomes free of difficulties, but because we are no longer carrying the weight of those difficulties by ourselves. When we take Jesus' yoke upon us, we are aligning ourselves with His strength, His wisdom, and His guidance. He doesn't promise to take away every hardship, but He does promise to walk with us through every trial, to carry the weight that is too heavy for us, and to give us the grace to endure whatever comes our way.

Jesus also calls us to "learn of me" in this verse. This means that when we take His yoke, we are not just sharing the load—we are entering into a relationship of learning and growth. Jesus is the perfect teacher, and when we walk with Him, we learn how to live in a way that is in alignment with God's will. We learn from His example of humility, gentleness, and love. We learn to trust God more deeply, to love others more selflessly, and to walk in obedience to His commands. Jesus doesn't just want to lighten our load—He wants to transform our hearts and our lives. He wants to teach us how to live in the freedom and peace that come from being fully surrendered to God. This is why His yoke is easy and His burden is light—because when we walk with Him, we are not living in our own strength but in the strength that He provides.

Taking Jesus' yoke upon us also means that we are submitting to His authority. A yoke is something that binds two beings together, and when we take Jesus' yoke, we are choosing to bind ourselves to Him, to walk in step with Him, and to follow His lead. This is not a burden—it is a gift. Jesus' leadership is gentle, loving, and full of grace. He doesn't lead us with harshness or cruelty—He leads us with compassion, understanding, and patience. To be yoked with Jesus means that we are no longer walking our own path, trying to figure things out on our own—it means that we are walking with Him, following His guidance, and trusting that He knows the best way forward. It means that we don't have to carry the burdens of life alone because we are yoked together with the One who is all-powerful, all-loving, and all-knowing.

One of the most beautiful aspects of taking Jesus' yoke upon us is the rest that it brings to our souls. Jesus specifically says in Matthew 11:29, "you will find rest for your souls." This rest is not just a temporary break from the busyness of life—it is a deep, lasting peace that comes from knowing that we are not alone, that we are not carrying the weight of the world on our shoulders, and that we are walking with the Savior who loves us, cares for us, and is always with us. This rest is the antidote to the anxiety, stress, and exhaustion that so many of us carry. It is the rest that comes from knowing that we don't have to have all the answers, that we don't have to solve every problem, and that we can trust Jesus to guide us, to provide for us, and to carry us through every challenge. When we take Jesus' yoke upon us, we find the rest that our souls have been longing for.

But taking Jesus' yoke also requires trust. It requires us to trust that His way is better than our way, that His wisdom is greater than our understanding, and that His love for us is deeper than we can imagine. It requires us to let go of our need to control, to fix, and to strive, and to instead rest in His guidance, His provision, and His care. This kind of trust is not easy—it goes against our natural inclination to rely on ourselves, to try to handle everything on our own. But when we trust Jesus enough to take His yoke upon us, we discover that His way is truly better. We find that His grace is sufficient for every challenge, that His strength is made perfect in our weakness (2 Corinthians 12:9), and that His peace surpasses all understanding (Philippians 4:7).

Taking Jesus' yoke upon us also means learning to walk in step with Him. Just as two animals yoked together must walk in sync, we must learn to walk in sync with Jesus. This means slowing down when He calls us to slow down, and moving forward when He leads us forward. It means learning to listen to His voice, to follow His lead, and to trust His timing. So often, we rush ahead of God, trying to make things happen in our own strength, or we lag behind, fearful of stepping into what He is calling us to do. But when we take Jesus' yoke upon us, we learn to walk in step with Him, to trust His pace, and to follow His guidance. This brings a sense of peace and rhythm to our lives, as we learn to live in alignment with God's will, rather than striving in our own strength.

Jesus' invitation to take His yoke upon us is an invitation to live in the freedom and joy that come from being in relationship with Him. It is an invitation to let go of the burdens that have been weighing us down—whether they are the burdens of fear, worry, guilt, or shame—and to find rest in His love and grace. It is an invitation to learn from Him, to grow in our understanding of who He is, and to be transformed by His presence in our lives. Jesus' yoke is easy and His burden is light because it is rooted in His love for us. He doesn't ask us to carry the weight of the world on our shoulders—He asks us to trust Him, to walk with Him, and to let Him carry the heavy burdens for us.

As you continue through "Answer the Call – 31 Days of Bold Biblical Action", let this call to "take" Jesus' yoke upon you be an invitation to experience the peace, rest, and freedom that come from walking with Him. If you've been carrying heavy burdens—whether they are physical, emotional, or spiritual—now is the time to take them to Jesus. He is inviting you to take His yoke upon you, to let Him share the load, and to find rest for your soul. You don't have to carry the weight of life on your own—Jesus is offering to walk with you, to guide you, and to give you the strength you need.

Take His yoke, and learn from Him. Learn how to live in the peace that comes from trusting Him. Learn how to love others as He loves you. Learn how to walk in humility, grace, and compassion. Learn how to surrender your burdens to Him and to rest in His presence. Take His yoke, and experience the joy of walking in step with the Savior who loves you more than you can imagine.

Take His yoke, and let go of the things that have been weighing you down. Let go of the fear, the worry, the anxiety, and the stress. Let go of the need to control, to fix, and to strive. Take His yoke, and trust that He will guide you, provide for you, and give you the strength you need for whatever lies ahead.

Take His yoke, and find rest for your soul. This is not just a temporary rest—it is the deep, lasting rest that comes from knowing that you are loved, cared for, and held by the One who created you. It is the rest that comes from walking in step with Jesus, from trusting His heart, and from allowing His love to carry you through every challenge.

Take His yoke, and let Jesus lead you into the life that He has for you—a life that is full of His peace, His joy, and His love. Take His yoke, and experience the transformation that comes from being in relationship with Him. Take His yoke, and learn what it means to live in the freedom and grace that He offers.

Take His yoke, and find the rest, peace, and joy that your soul has been longing for.

Chapter 27 – Speak

In the twenty-seventh call to action from "Answer the Call – 31 Days of Bold Biblical Action", we are challenged with one of the most profound and important commands in Scripture: "But speaking the truth in love, may grow up into him in all things, which is the head, even Christ:" (Ephesians 4:15). These words call us to a balance that is often difficult to maintain—truth and love, both essential, intertwined, and inseparable in the way we communicate with others. Speaking the truth is critical because it honors God's Word, upholds integrity, and fosters genuine relationships. But truth without love can become harsh, critical, or even damaging. On the other hand, love without truth can become shallow, enabling, or even misleading. Jesus embodies both perfect truth and perfect love, and as followers of Christ, we are called to reflect His character in our words and actions. To "speak the truth in love" is not just a suggestion for how we communicate—it is a foundational principle for how we live as believers, how we interact with others, and how we represent Christ in the world.

To speak the truth in love means that we are committed to honesty, even when the truth is hard to hear or difficult to say. It means that we don't shy away from speaking the truth out of fear of conflict or discomfort, but we do so with a heart that is motivated by love. Love is what makes the truth bearable, and truth is what gives love depth and substance. When we speak the truth in love, we are not using our words to tear others down or to win arguments—we are using our words to build others up, to encourage growth, and to help others see the truth of God's Word and His ways. Speaking the truth in love requires wisdom, patience, and compassion. It requires us to consider not just what we are saying, but how we are saying it and why we are saying it. Are we speaking out of love, or are we speaking out of pride, anger, or a desire to be right?

One of the most challenging aspects of speaking the truth in love is knowing when and how to speak. There are times when the truth needs to be spoken boldly and clearly, and there are times when the truth needs to be spoken gently and patiently. Wisdom comes from discerning the right approach in each situation, understanding that every person and every circumstance is different. When we speak the truth in love, we are mindful of the impact our words will have on others. We are sensitive to their feelings, their struggles, and their perspectives, and we seek to communicate in a way that honors them and points them toward Christ. This doesn't mean that we water down the truth or avoid difficult conversations—it means that we approach those conversations with humility, grace, and a genuine desire for the other person's well-being.

Speaking the truth in love also means that we are committed to building relationships that are rooted in honesty and transparency. Love does not allow us to lie, to manipulate, or to deceive. Love requires us to be truthful, even when it is uncomfortable or inconvenient. But the truth spoken in love is not harsh or condemning—it is kind, gentle, and redemptive. It seeks to heal, not to harm; to restore, not to break down. When we speak the truth in love, we are seeking the best for the other person, even if that means having a difficult conversation or addressing something that needs to change. The goal is always to build up, to encourage, and to help others grow in their faith and their relationship with God.

At the heart of speaking the truth in love is the desire to reflect the character of Christ. Jesus is the ultimate example of truth and love perfectly balanced. Throughout His ministry, Jesus never compromised the truth, but He always spoke it with love. Whether He was teaching, correcting, or comforting, His words were filled with both truth and grace. He spoke the truth to the Pharisees when they were hypocritical, but He did so with the hope of bringing them to repentance. He spoke the truth to the woman caught in adultery, but He did so with compassion, offering her forgiveness and a new start. In every situation, Jesus spoke the truth in a way that pointed people toward God's love and grace. As His followers, we are called to do the same.

When we speak the truth in love, we are choosing to love others enough to be honest with them, even when it's hard. It's not always easy to tell the truth, especially when the truth might hurt or cause discomfort. But love compels us to speak the truth because we care about the other person's spiritual growth and well-being. It's important to remember that speaking the truth in love is not about trying to "fix" someone or to prove that we are right—it's about helping them see the truth of God's Word and His heart for them. It's about encouraging them to walk in the light, to grow in their faith, and to become more like Christ.

At the same time, speaking the truth in love requires us to be humble. We must recognize that we don't have all the answers and that we are still growing and learning ourselves. When we speak the truth in love, we do so from a place of humility, acknowledging our own need for God's grace and truth. This humility allows us to approach others with a heart that is open, compassionate, and willing to listen. It's not about being judgmental or self-righteous—it's about coming alongside others, walking with them in their journey of faith, and encouraging them to grow closer to God.

One of the most powerful ways we can speak the truth in love is through our everyday conversations. Whether we are talking with family, friends, coworkers, or strangers, our words have the power to build up or tear down, to bring life or to cause harm. When we choose to speak the truth in love, we are choosing to use our words to bring healing, encouragement, and hope. We are choosing to speak words that reflect the heart of God, words that point people to His love and grace. This doesn't mean that every conversation will be easy or that every truth we speak will be well-received. But when we speak with love, we can trust that God will use our words to accomplish His purposes.

Speaking the truth in love is also about being willing to have difficult conversations when necessary. There are times when we need to confront sin, address wrong behavior, or challenge harmful attitudes. These conversations can be uncomfortable, but they are necessary for growth and healing. When we speak the truth in love in these situations, we do so with the goal of helping the other person come to a place of repentance and restoration. We don't confront out of anger or frustration—we confront out of a desire to see the other person set free from the things that are holding them back. And we do so with love, knowing that it is only through God's grace and truth that true transformation can happen.

But speaking the truth in love is not just about correcting others—it's also about being open to hearing the truth ourselves. We need to be willing to listen when others speak the truth to us, even if it's hard to hear. We need to be humble enough to receive correction, to admit when we are wrong, and to allow God to use the truth spoken by others to shape us and help us grow. This is a two-way street—just as we are called to speak the truth in love, we are also called to receive the truth in love. When we do, we create an environment of trust, openness, and mutual respect in our relationships, where both truth and love can flourish.

Another important aspect of speaking the truth in love is knowing when to speak and when to remain silent. There are times when the most loving thing we can do is speak the truth, and there are times when the most loving thing we can do is to listen and wait. This requires wisdom and discernment, as well as a deep reliance on the Holy Spirit. Sometimes, the truth needs to be spoken immediately, and sometimes, it needs to be spoken after prayer and reflection. There are moments when silence can speak louder than words, and there are moments when words are necessary to bring clarity and healing. The key is to be sensitive to the leading of the Holy Spirit, to be rooted in God's Word, and to always speak from a heart of love.

When we speak the truth in love, we are participating in the work of building up the body of Christ. Ephesians 4:15 goes on to say that speaking the truth in love helps us "grow up in every way into him who is the head, into Christ." Our words have the power to help others grow in their faith, to encourage them in their walk with God, and to strengthen the body of Christ as a whole. This is a sacred responsibility, and it requires us to be intentional about how we use our words. We are called to speak words that bring life, hope, and healing—words that reflect the love and truth of Jesus.

As you continue through "Answer the Call – 31 Days of Bold Biblical Action", let this call to "speak the truth in love" be an invitation to use your words to reflect the heart of Christ. If there are conversations you've been avoiding or truths you've been hesitant to speak, now is the time to step out in faith and speak the truth in love. Trust that God will give you the wisdom, the words, and the grace you need to communicate in a way that honors Him and builds others up.

Speak the truth in love, and watch as God uses your words to bring healing, restoration, and transformation in the lives of others. Speak the truth in love, and experience the freedom that comes from living in honesty, integrity, and grace. Speak the truth in love, and let your words be a reflection of the love of Christ, pointing others to His truth and His heart. Speak the truth in love, and trust that God will use your words to accomplish His purposes and to build up His kingdom.

Speak the truth in love, and know that your words have the power to bring life, to bring hope, and to bring healing. Speak the truth in love, and let your conversations be filled with grace, kindness, and compassion. Speak the truth in love, and let your words reflect the character of Christ, who is both full of grace and full of truth. Speak the truth in love, and watch as God uses your words to make a lasting impact on the lives of those around you.

Chapter 28 – Come

In the twenty-eighth call to action from "Answer the Call – 31 Days of Bold Biblical Action", we hear one of the most tender and inviting promises from Jesus: "Come unto me, all *ye* that labour and are heavy laden, and I will give you rest." (Matthew 11:28). These words are filled with compassion, understanding, and hope as Jesus extends an invitation to every person who feels worn out, burdened, or overwhelmed by the struggles of life. He sees our exhaustion, the weight of our worries, our fears, and the heaviness that so many of us carry day after day. Whether it's the pressure to succeed, the strain of relationships, financial struggles, health challenges, or the spiritual battles we face, Jesus knows the load we are carrying. He invites us to come to Him, not because He wants something from us, but because He wants to give us something: rest. This isn't just physical rest—it's soul-deep, life-transforming rest. It's the kind of peace and relief that comes when we release the heavy burdens we've been carrying and allow Jesus to carry them for us.

When Jesus says, "Come unto me," He is inviting us to step away from the endless striving, the feelings of inadequacy, and the pressure to handle everything on our own. He's calling us to let go of the belief that we have to have it all figured out, that we have to be strong enough, or that we need to be perfect. In this invitation, Jesus is offering us a chance to lay down our burdens at His feet and to find relief in His presence. He isn't offering a temporary escape or a quick fix; He's offering lasting peace and rest for our souls. This is an invitation to come as you are, no matter how tired, broken, or burdened you feel, and to find the comfort and healing that only He can provide.

Jesus' invitation is open to everyone who is weary and burdened. He doesn't discriminate or limit His invitation to those who have it all together. He specifically calls out to those who are struggling, those who are tired, those who are weighed down by the pressures and difficulties of life. This includes all of us, because at some point, every one of us experiences the weight of life's challenges. Whether we are burdened by the weight of sin, by the expectations of others, by grief, or by the constant demands of daily life, Jesus' invitation is for us. He knows our struggles, and He offers Himself as the solution. He doesn't just offer advice or encouragement—He offers His very presence, His love, and His strength.

To "come unto me" means to draw near to Jesus, to approach Him with open hearts and open hands, ready to receive the rest and relief that He is offering. It's an invitation to step away from the busyness, the distractions, and the constant noise of the world and to focus on Him. When we come to Jesus, we are invited to stop striving, stop trying to carry everything on our own, and instead, to rest in His love and grace. Coming to Jesus means trusting Him with our burdens, believing that He cares for us, and knowing that He is more than capable of handling whatever we are facing. It's an act of faith, where we acknowledge our own limitations and trust in His limitless power and grace.

But coming to Jesus also requires humility. It means admitting that we are not strong enough to carry the burdens we've been trying to bear on our own. It means recognizing that we need Him, that we can't do it all by ourselves, and that we need His help, His strength, and His grace. This kind of humility goes against our natural inclination to be self-sufficient, to appear strong, and to handle everything on our own. But Jesus invites us to lay down our pride, to be honest about our struggles, and to come to Him with our weaknesses and our burdens. He promises that when we do, we will find rest. This rest isn't just a temporary relief from our problems—it's a deep, soul-satisfying rest that comes from being in His presence, knowing that we are loved, cared for, and never alone.

One of the most beautiful aspects of this invitation is that Jesus doesn't expect us to fix ourselves before we come to Him. He doesn't ask us to get everything in order or to clean up our messes before we approach Him. He invites us to come just as we are, with all of our brokenness, all of our failures, and all of our burdens. He is not put off by our mess—He welcomes us with open arms. When we come to Jesus, we don't have to pretend that we have it all together. We can come with our doubts, our fears, and our weariness, and He will meet us right where we are. His love is not conditional on our performance—it is freely given, and it is enough to carry us through even the darkest and most difficult times.

Jesus' invitation to come to Him is also a call to find our identity and our worth in Him. So many of us carry the burden of trying to prove ourselves—whether it's through our work, our relationships, or our achievements. We feel the constant pressure to be good enough, to do enough, and to measure up to the expectations of others or even our own expectations. But Jesus calls us to lay down that burden and to find our identity in Him. When we come to Jesus, we are reminded that our worth is not based on what we do, but on who we are in Him. We are loved, we are accepted, and we are enough because He says we are. In His presence, we find the freedom to let go of the need to perform and to rest in the truth that we are deeply loved and fully known by the God who created us.

Coming to Jesus also means finding peace in the midst of life's storms. Jesus never promised that we would have a life free of trouble or difficulty, but He did promise that we could find peace in Him. In John 16:33, He says, "In this world you will have trouble. But take heart! I have overcome the world." When we come to Jesus, we are not promised a life without challenges, but we are promised His presence, His peace, and His strength to carry us through those challenges. No matter what we are facing—whether it's grief, anxiety, fear, or uncertainty—Jesus invites us to come to Him and to find peace in the midst of the storm. His peace is not the absence of trouble, but the presence of His love, His comfort, and His assurance that He is with us, and He is in control.

Jesus' invitation to "come unto me" is also a call to intimacy with Him. It's not just about finding relief from our burdens—it's about entering into a relationship with the One who loves us more than we can imagine. Jesus doesn't just want to take our burdens away—He wants to walk with us, to know us, and to be known by us. When we come to Jesus, we are invited into a deep, personal relationship with the God of the universe. We are invited to experience His love, His grace, and His presence in a way that transforms our lives. This relationship is not distant or formal—it is intimate, personal, and filled with love. Jesus is not a distant Savior—He is a close, personal friend who walks with us through every moment of our lives.

But coming to Jesus also requires surrender. It means letting go of our need to control, to fix, and to handle everything on our own. It means trusting that

Jesus knows what is best for us, and that His plans are better than our own. This kind of surrender is not easy—it goes against our natural desire to be in control. But when we surrender to Jesus, we find that His way is always better. We find that His grace is sufficient, that His strength is made perfect in our weakness, and that His love is more than enough to carry us through whatever we are facing. When we come to Jesus and surrender our burdens to Him, we find freedom, peace, and rest.

As you continue through "Answer the Call – 31 Days of Bold Biblical Action", let this call to "come" be an invitation to experience the rest and peace that Jesus offers. If you are carrying heavy burdens—whether they are physical, emotional, or spiritual—now is the time to bring them to Jesus. He is inviting you to come to Him, to lay down your burdens, and to find rest in His presence. You don't have to carry the weight of life on your own—Jesus is offering to walk with you, to carry your burdens, and to give you the rest that your soul needs.

Come to Jesus, and find the peace that comes from knowing that you are not alone. Come to Jesus, and find the rest that comes from letting go of the need to control and trusting in His love and grace. Come to Jesus, and experience the freedom that comes from being in relationship with the Savior who loves you more than you can imagine.

Come to Jesus, and let go of the burdens that have been weighing you down. Let go of the fear, the worry, the stress, and the anxiety. Come to Jesus, and find the rest that your soul has been longing for. Come to Jesus, and experience the joy, peace, and freedom that come from walking in relationship with Him.

Come to Jesus, and know that His invitation is open to you, no matter where you are, no matter what you've been through, and no matter how heavy your burdens are. Come to Jesus, and find the rest that only He can provide. Come to Jesus, and let His love and grace transform your life.

Chapter 29 - Fear Not

In the twenty-ninth call to action from "Answer the Call – 31 Days of Bold Biblical Action", we are confronted with one of the most comforting and powerful promises from God: "Fear thou not; for I am with thee: be not dismayed; for I am thy God: I will strengthen thee; yea, I will help thee; yea, I will uphold thee with the right hand of my righteousness." (Isaiah 41:10). These simple yet profound words hold the key to overcoming one of the most universal human emotions—fear. Fear can grip our hearts, paralyze us, and keep us from living fully and freely. Whether it's the fear of the unknown, fear of failure, fear of loss, fear of rejection, or fear of the future, we all face moments when fear threatens to overwhelm us. But in this verse, God speaks directly to the heart of our fear and offers the ultimate antidote: His presence. "Fear not, for I am with thee" is more than just a command to stop being afraid—it's a promise that we are never alone, that the God of the universe is with us, walking beside us, protecting us, guiding us, and giving us the strength we need to face whatever comes our way.

When God says "Fear not," He isn't dismissing our fears or telling us that we should never feel afraid. He knows that fear is a natural human response to danger, uncertainty, and difficulty. Instead, He is reminding us that we don't have to be controlled or overcome by fear because we are not facing life's challenges on our own. The promise "I am with thee" is a declaration of God's unwavering presence in our lives. No matter what we are going through, no matter how dark or frightening the situation may seem, God is with us. He is not a distant or indifferent God—He is Immanuel, God with us, right here in the midst of our fear, our pain, our uncertainty. His presence is the reason we can move forward with courage and confidence, knowing that we are not alone.

To truly understand the power of this promise, we must grasp the significance of God's presence in our lives. God is not just with us in a general sense—He is intimately involved in every detail of our lives. He knows our struggles, our doubts, our weaknesses, and our fears, and He cares deeply about them. When He says, "I am with thee," He is not offering us a vague sense of comfort—He is offering us His very presence, His strength, His protection, and His peace. This means that whatever we are facing, whether it's a health crisis, a financial struggle, a broken relationship, or a difficult decision, we can face it with confidence because God is with us. He is not just watching from a distance—He is actively involved, working on our behalf, and walking with us every step of the way.

The command "Fear not" is repeated throughout Scripture, and it is almost always accompanied by a reminder of God's presence or His promises. This shows us that the key to overcoming fear is not found in our own strength or abilities, but in trusting God's presence and His promises. We don't have to be fearless because we are strong—we can be fearless because God is strong, and He is with us. The truth is, we are often weak, and life's challenges can feel overwhelming. But when we focus on God's presence, we are reminded that we don't have to face those challenges alone. God's strength becomes our strength, His wisdom becomes our guide, and His peace guards our hearts and minds.

One of the most comforting aspects of this promise is that God's presence is constant. He doesn't come and go based on our circumstances or our performance. He is with us in the good times and the bad, in the moments of joy and the moments of pain. Whether we feel His presence or not, the truth remains: God is with us. When we are afraid, it can be easy to feel isolated or abandoned, but God's promise is that He will never leave us or forsake us (Deuteronomy 31:6). His presence is not dependent on how we feel—His presence is a constant, unchanging reality. This means that even in our darkest moments, even when fear seems overwhelming, we can hold onto the truth that God is with us, and He is faithful.

"Fear not, for I am with thee" is also a reminder that we can trust God's character. God is not just with us—He is for us. He is good, loving, and faithful, and He is working all things together for our good (Romans 8:28). When we are afraid, it's often because we don't know what the future holds or because we feel out of control. But God knows the future, and He is in control. We may not understand why things are happening the way they are, but we can trust that God does, and that He has a plan for our lives that is good and perfect.

Trusting in God's character means believing that even when we can't see the way forward, God is already there, guiding us and making a way for us. His presence gives us the courage to keep moving forward, even when we are afraid.

Fear often thrives in uncertainty, but God's promise to be with us gives us the assurance we need to face the unknown. Whether we are stepping into a new season of life, facing a difficult decision, or walking through a season of loss, God's presence is our anchor. He is the solid rock on which we stand, and His presence gives us stability in the midst of life's storms. The future may be uncertain, but God is not. He is the same yesterday, today, and forever (Hebrews 13:8), and His presence is our constant source of peace and strength. When we are tempted to be overwhelmed by fear, we can remind ourselves that God is with us, and He is greater than anything we may face.

God's presence also brings peace. In Philippians 4:6-7, we are told to "be anxious for nothing, but in everything by prayer and supplication with thanksgiving, let your requests be made known to God. And the peace of God, which surpasses all understanding, will guard your hearts and minds through Christ Jesus." When we bring our fears to God and trust in His presence, He replaces our anxiety with His peace. This peace is not based on our circumstances—it is based on the reality of God's presence with us. It is a peace that transcends our understanding, a peace that guards our hearts and minds, even in the midst of fear and uncertainty.

The command to "Fear not" is not just about our personal struggles—it is also a call to live courageously for God's kingdom. Fear can keep us from stepping out in faith, from pursuing the calling God has placed on our lives, or from sharing the gospel with others. But when we trust that God is with us, we are freed from the paralysis of fear, and we are empowered to live boldly for Him. Whether it's sharing our faith with a friend, stepping into a new ministry, or standing up for what is right in the face of opposition, God's presence gives us the courage we need to live out our faith with boldness and confidence. We don't have to fear failure, rejection, or persecution because God is with us, and His presence is enough.

God's promise, "I am with thee," also means that we have access to His wisdom and guidance. When we are facing difficult decisions or uncertain circumstances, we don't have to navigate them on our own. God is with us, and He is ready to guide us, to give us wisdom, and to show us the way forward.

In James 1:5, we are told that if we lack wisdom, we should ask God, who gives generously to all without finding fault. God's presence means that we can approach Him with confidence, knowing that He will give us the wisdom and guidance we need to make the right choices.

In moments of fear, we are also reminded that God's presence is protective. Psalm 91:1-2 says, "He who dwells in the secret place of the Most High shall abide under the shadow of the Almighty. I will say of the LORD, 'He is my refuge and my fortress; my God, in Him I will trust.'" God is our refuge and fortress, a place of safety and protection in times of trouble. When we are afraid, we can run to Him, knowing that He will shelter us and protect us from harm. His presence is a shield around us, and no matter what we face, we can rest in the assurance that God is watching over us, guarding us, and keeping us safe in His care.

As you continue through "Answer the Call – 31 Days of Bold Biblical Action", let this call to "Fear not" be an invitation to live in the peace and confidence that comes from knowing that God is with you. If you are facing fears—whether they are fears about the future, fears about your circumstances, or fears about your own inadequacies—now is the time to bring them to God. He is with you, and He is ready to give you the courage, strength, and peace you need to move forward.

Fear not, for God is with you. Trust in His presence, rely on His strength, and rest in His love. Fear not, for the God who created the universe is walking with you every step of the way. Fear not, for His presence is your shield, your refuge, and your strength. Fear not, for He is faithful, and He will never leave you or forsake you. Fear not, for the God who is with you is greater than any fear you may face.

Fear not, and live in the freedom that comes from knowing that you are never alone. Fear not, and step out in faith, trusting that God is with you, guiding you, and working all things together for your good. Fear not, and experience the peace that surpasses all understanding, the peace that comes from resting in the presence of the One who holds you in His hands.

Fear not, for God is with you, and His presence is all you need.

Chapter 30 – Sing

In the thirtieth call to action from "Answer the Call – 31 Days of Bold Biblical Action", we are invited into one of the most joyful and powerful expressions of worship: "O sing unto the LORD a new song: sing unto the LORD, all the earth." (Psalm 96:1). This simple yet profound command reaches deep into the heart of our faith and reminds us that singing is not just a ritual, but a spiritual act of worship that connects us to the very presence of God. It's more than just words put to music—it's the outpouring of our hearts in gratitude, love, and praise for the One who created us, who loves us, and who redeems us. To "sing unto the Lord" is to lift up our voices in worship, declaring His goodness, His faithfulness, and His glory. It's an invitation for every person, no matter their background or situation, to join in the eternal song of praise to the Creator of the universe. Whether we feel like singing or not, whether life is going well or we're walking through the darkest valleys, this command calls us to sing because it's not based on our circumstances—it's based on who God is, and He is always worthy of our praise.

When we sing to the Lord, we are participating in something that goes far beyond ourselves. Psalm 96:1 says, "Sing unto the LORD, all the earth." This call to sing is not limited to just a few people—it's a call for all of creation to join in the worship of our Creator. The mountains, the rivers, the trees, the animals, and every human being are invited to lift up their voices in praise to God. Singing connects us to the whole of creation, reminding us that we are part of something much bigger than ourselves. Our voices join with the chorus of heaven and earth, declaring the majesty and glory of God. When we sing, we are joining in the eternal song that has been sung since the beginning of time—a song of praise, worship, and adoration for the God who is holy, loving, and just.

Singing unto the Lord is also a way of expressing the deepest emotions of our hearts. There are times in life when words alone cannot express the depth of our joy, gratitude, or even our pain. In those moments, singing becomes a powerful way to communicate with God, to pour out our hearts before Him, and to offer up everything we are feeling in a way that words alone cannot capture. Whether it's a song of joy and celebration or a song of lament and sorrow, singing allows us to be honest with God, to bring Him our full selves—our hopes, our fears, our victories, and our struggles. It's an act of vulnerability, where we open our hearts to God and invite Him into our deepest emotions. Singing is not just for the good times—it's for every season of life, because no matter what we're going through, God is worthy of our praise, and He meets us in our songs.

One of the most beautiful things about singing unto the Lord is that it changes us. When we sing, we are not just declaring truths about God—we are reminding ourselves of those truths. We are lifting our eyes from our circumstances and focusing them on the One who is greater than anything we face. Singing shifts our perspective, helping us to see beyond our immediate struggles and challenges and to remember that God is in control, that He is faithful, and that His love for us never fails. It's hard to remain focused on our worries or fears when we are singing about God's goodness, His power, and His promises. In this way, singing is an act of faith—it's choosing to praise God, even when we don't feel like it, trusting that He is still worthy of our worship and that He is working all things together for our good.

Singing unto the Lord is also a way of building up our faith. The songs we sing often contain truths from Scripture, reminding us of who God is and what He has done. When we sing, we are declaring those truths over our lives, allowing them to sink deep into our hearts and strengthen our faith. Songs like "Amazing Grace," "How Great Thou Art," and "Great Is Thy Faithfulness" remind us of God's character, His love, and His promises. They help us to remember His faithfulness in the past, His presence with us in the present, and His promises for the future. Singing these truths out loud reinforces them in our minds and hearts, giving us the strength and courage to face whatever challenges lie ahead. Singing is not just an emotional expression—it's a spiritual discipline that helps us to focus on God's truth and to build our faith.

There is also something incredibly powerful about singing in community. When we gather together as the body of Christ and lift our voices in song, we are united in worship. It's a reminder that we are not alone in our faith—we are part of a larger family of believers who are all worshiping the same God. There is a special kind of strength and encouragement that comes from singing with others, from hearing their voices join with ours in praise. In those moments, we are reminded that we are not walking this journey of faith alone—our brothers and sisters in Christ are walking with us, and together, we are lifting up the name of Jesus. Singing together is a powerful way of building community, of encouraging one another, and of proclaiming the greatness of God to the world around us.

Singing unto the Lord is also a way of proclaiming the gospel. The songs we sing often contain the message of God's love and salvation, and when we sing them, we are declaring that message to the world. Psalm 96:2 says, "Sing to the LORD, bless his name; tell of his salvation from day to day." Our songs are a way of sharing the good news of Jesus Christ, of telling the world about the God who loves them, who came to save them, and who invites them into a relationship with Him. When we sing, we are not just worshiping for ourselves—we are proclaiming the truth of the gospel to those around us. Our songs have the power to inspire, to encourage, and to draw people to God. They are a testimony to the greatness of God and His love for all people.

Even in times of struggle or hardship, singing unto the Lord is an act of faith and surrender. There are moments when life feels overwhelming, when it feels like there is nothing to sing about, yet even in those moments, God invites us to sing. It's in those times of darkness and difficulty that singing becomes an act of defiance against the enemy, a declaration that no matter what we are facing, we will continue to praise God. Singing in the midst of hardship is a powerful way of declaring that our hope is not in our circumstances but in the God who holds our lives in His hands. It's choosing to trust that God is still good, even when life is hard, and that His love for us never changes, even when everything else does.

One of the reasons singing is so powerful is that it allows us to engage with God on multiple levels—emotionally, spiritually, and even physically. When we sing, we are using our voices, our breath, and our bodies to express our love and worship for God. It's a way of fully engaging with God, of offering Him not just our words but our whole selves. Singing involves our hearts, our minds, and our bodies, and in doing so, it allows us to experience God's presence in a deeper and more personal way. There is something about singing that draws us closer to God, that helps us to connect with Him on a level that goes beyond words. It's a way of expressing our love for Him, our gratitude for His grace, and our awe at His majesty.

Singing unto the Lord is also a way of releasing our burdens. There is something incredibly freeing about lifting up our voices in worship, about letting go of the things that are weighing us down and choosing to focus on God's goodness and faithfulness. When we sing, we are reminded that God is bigger than our problems, that He is in control, and that He cares for us. Singing helps us to shift our focus from our worries to God's promises, from our struggles to His strength. It's a way of surrendering our burdens to Him and trusting that He will carry them for us. In this way, singing becomes a form of prayer—a way of bringing our hearts to God and finding peace in His presence.

As you continue through "Answer the Call – 31 Days of Bold Biblical Action", let this call to "Sing unto the LORD" be an invitation to worship God with your whole heart. Whether you are in a season of joy or a season of sorrow, whether you feel like singing or not, remember that God is always worthy of your praise. Lift up your voice and sing to Him, trusting that as you do, He will meet you in that place of worship. Sing to the Lord, and allow His presence to fill your heart with peace, joy, and hope. Sing, knowing that your songs are a powerful way of expressing your love for God, of building your faith, and of proclaiming His greatness to the world.

Sing unto the Lord, and let your voice join with the chorus of heaven and earth in declaring the majesty and glory of God. Sing, and allow the truth of God's Word to sink deep into your heart, strengthening your faith and encouraging your spirit. Sing, and experience the freedom that comes from surrendering your burdens to God and trusting in His love and grace. Sing, and know that your songs are not just for you—they are a testimony to the greatness of God and a proclamation of His love and salvation to the world.

Sing unto the Lord, and experience the joy that comes from worshiping the God who created you, who loves you, and who has redeemed you. Sing, and let your heart be filled with gratitude for all that God has done. Sing, and know that no matter what you are facing, God is with you, and He is worthy of your praise. Sing unto the Lord, all the earth, and let His name be glorified in your life, in your community, and in the world around you. Sing, for God is good, and His love endures forever.

Chapter 31 - Give Thanks

In the thirty-first and final call to action from "Answer the Call – 31 Days of Bold Biblical Action", we are given one of the most transformative commands in Scripture: "In every thing give thanks: for this is the will of God in Christ Jesus concerning you." (1 Thessalonians 5:18). These words challenge us to live a life of gratitude, not just in the good times, but in every circumstance—whether we are experiencing joy or sorrow, success or failure, abundance or need. Giving thanks in all things is not just a matter of saying polite "thank you's" when life is going well; it's a radical act of faith that transforms how we see the world, how we experience life's ups and downs, and how we connect with God. Gratitude in the face of trials and difficulties is a powerful declaration that we trust in God's goodness and sovereignty, even when we don't understand what's happening. It's an expression of faith that says, "Lord, I may not see the whole picture, but I trust that You are working all things together for my good" (Romans 8:28).

Giving thanks in everything does not mean that we are thankful for the pain, the hardships, or the losses we face. It means that in the midst of those difficulties, we choose to focus on God's presence, His promises, and His faithfulness. It's about finding reasons to be grateful even when life feels overwhelming. When we give thanks in everything, we are choosing to see beyond our circumstances and to acknowledge that God is still with us, that He is still good, and that His love for us has not changed. Gratitude shifts our focus from what we lack to what we have, from what's wrong to what's right, and from what we can't control to the God who is in control of all things.

One of the most powerful aspects of giving thanks in everything is the way it changes our hearts. Gratitude has the power to transform our outlook on life. When we choose to be thankful, we are choosing joy over bitterness, hope over despair, and trust over fear. Gratitude opens our eyes to the blessings that are often hidden in the midst of our struggles—the small moments of grace, the unexpected kindnesses, the ways God is providing for us even in the hard times. It helps us to see that even in our darkest moments, there is still light. Even in our most difficult seasons, there is still reason to praise. Gratitude is a practice that, over time, reshapes our hearts and minds to focus more on God's goodness than on life's challenges.

When Paul wrote these words in 1 Thessalonians 5:18, "In everything give thanks," he wasn't writing from a place of comfort and ease. Paul knew hardship. He experienced imprisonment, persecution, shipwrecks, and countless trials for the sake of the gospel. And yet, he could still write these words because he had learned the secret of true gratitude—it's not about our circumstances, but about the God who is with us in those circumstances. Paul's life was marked by a deep trust in God's goodness and faithfulness, even when life didn't make sense. And that's what enabled him to give thanks in all things. He knew that no matter what he faced, God was still in control, and God's purposes would still prevail.

Gratitude is also a form of worship. When we give thanks, we are acknowledging that every good thing in our lives comes from God (James 1:17). We are recognizing His provision, His grace, and His blessings, and we are giving Him the glory for it all. When we thank God in every circumstance, we are lifting our eyes from our problems and focusing them on His greatness. We are reminding ourselves that He is bigger than any challenge we face, that His love is greater than any fear, and that His power is sufficient to carry us through even the most difficult times. In this way, gratitude becomes an act of trust and surrender. It's a way of saying, "God, I trust You. I believe that You are good, even when life is hard. I choose to thank You, because I know that You are with me, and You will never leave me."

Giving thanks in everything is also an act of obedience. The Bible doesn't suggest that we give thanks when we feel like it or when life is going our way—it commands us to give thanks in everything. This means that gratitude is not based on our emotions or circumstances, but on our decision to trust God. It's a choice we make, even when it's hard, even when we don't feel like it. And the beautiful thing is that when we choose to give thanks, even in the midst of pain or difficulty, something changes inside of us. Gratitude softens our hearts, opens us up to God's grace, and allows His peace to fill us in ways that nothing else can. It's a spiritual discipline that aligns our hearts with God's heart and reminds us of His constant presence and love.

There is incredible freedom in giving thanks. When we are caught up in fear, anxiety, or bitterness, our hearts feel heavy, and our perspective becomes clouded. But when we choose to thank God, even in the midst of uncertainty, it lifts the weight off our shoulders and allows us to rest in His goodness. Gratitude frees us from the trap of comparison, from the lie that we don't have enough, or that we aren't enough. It reminds us that we have everything we need in Christ, and that His grace is sufficient for us. When we give thanks, we stop focusing on what's missing or what's wrong, and we start focusing on the abundance of blessings that God has already given us.

Gratitude also strengthens our relationships. When we cultivate a heart of thankfulness, it spills over into how we treat others. We become more appreciative, more patient, and more forgiving. When we give thanks to God for the people in our lives, it helps us to see them through His eyes—with grace and love. Gratitude enables us to let go of petty grievances and to focus on the good in others. It reminds us that every person is a gift from God, and it encourages us to express our appreciation and love for them. When we are thankful, we become a source of encouragement and joy to those around us.

Gratitude also equips us to endure trials with grace. Life is full of challenges, and there will be times when it feels like everything is falling apart. In those moments, gratitude may feel like the last thing we want to practice. But it is precisely in those times that giving thanks becomes most powerful. When we choose to thank God in the midst of our pain, we are declaring that our hope is not in our circumstances but in Him. We are choosing to trust that He is working all things together for our good, even when we can't see it. And as we give thanks, we find that our perspective begins to shift. Instead of being consumed by our problems, we are reminded of God's faithfulness, His promises, and His presence with us in the storm.

Giving thanks in everything is a declaration of faith. It's saying, "God, I trust You, even when I don't understand. I believe that You are good, even when life is hard. I know that You are with me, even when I feel alone. I thank You because I know that You are working in ways I cannot see, and Your plans for me are good." This kind of faith-filled gratitude is a powerful witness to the world around us. It shows that our hope is not in this world, but in the God who created it. It testifies to the fact that we serve a God who is greater than any trial, who is faithful in every season, and who never leaves us.

As you continue through "Answer the Call – 31 Days of Bold Biblical Action", let this final call to "give thanks" be an invitation to live a life marked by gratitude. Whether you are in a season of abundance or a season of trial, choose to give thanks. Look for the ways that God is at work in your life, even in the small, quiet moments, and thank Him for His faithfulness. If you're struggling to find reasons to be thankful, start with the simple things—thank God for the breath in your lungs, for the beauty of creation, for the people in your life, and for His love that never fails. As you practice gratitude, you will find that it becomes easier to see God's hand in every circumstance.

Give thanks in everything, and watch as your heart is transformed. Give thanks, and experience the joy and peace that come from focusing on God's goodness, rather than your problems. Give thanks, and let your faith be strengthened as you trust in God's promises. Give thanks, and see how gratitude opens your eyes to the countless blessings that surround you every day. Give thanks in everything, for this is God's will for you in Christ Jesus.

Give thanks, and let your heart overflow with praise for the God who loves you, who is with you, and who is working all things together for your good. Give thanks, and allow that gratitude to shape how you see the world, how you interact with others, and how you experience life's ups and downs. Give thanks, and let your life be a testimony to the power of gratitude—a life that is not defined by circumstances, but by trust in the God who is always faithful.

In everything, give thanks. And in doing so, you will find that gratitude is not just a response to life's blessings—it is a way of life that brings joy, peace, and deeper connection to the God who gives us all we need.

Conclusion

As we reach the conclusion of "Answer the Call – 31 Days of Bold Biblical Action", this journey through Scripture has been more than just a 31-day challenge—it has been a spiritual awakening, a call to live out your faith with passion, purpose, and persistence. Each day, through the power of action-packed verbs like seek, pray, forgive, trust, and rejoice, you have taken steps to transform your life from a passive belief system to an active, vibrant walk with Christ. This book is not meant to be an end in itself but a launching point for a lifetime of bold, faith-filled living. Now that you have spent 31 days answering God's call to action, the question remains: What will you do next? How will you continue to walk with the Lord, not just today, but every day?

The truth is, the Christian life is a continual journey, not a destination you arrive at after 31 days. These past weeks have laid the foundation, showing you what it means to live a life that is not just about knowing the Word, but doing it. James 1:22 reminds us to be "doers of the word, and not hearers only," and that command continues long after this book ends. The verbs you've practiced—whether they were calls to love, serve, trust, or give thanks—are not temporary actions but lifelong practices that shape who you are as a follower of Christ. The challenge now is to carry these lessons forward, to continue living with the same intentionality and commitment, knowing that every step you take in obedience brings you closer to the heart of God.

Walking with the Lord is not about perfection; it's about persistence. There will be days when you stumble, days when the call to forgive feels too difficult, or the command to rejoice seems impossible in the face of trials. But that's exactly when you must dig deeper into the lessons learned in these 31 days. You must remember that each verb was not just an isolated command but a reflection of God's character and His promises to you. When He calls you to trust, He is inviting you to lean into His faithfulness. When He calls you to pray, He is reminding you that He is always listening, always near. When He calls you to love, He is showing you that His love for you is the source from which all your love for others flows. This journey is about trusting in His strength, not your own, and continuing to say yes to His call every single day.

The Christian walk is a daily decision to keep moving forward, to keep answering the call even when the road gets tough. It's about remaining steadfast in your commitment to seek God first in everything. It's about choosing to serve others, to speak the truth in love, and to give thanks in all circumstances. These are not just one-time actions—they are the building blocks of a life devoted to Christ. As you continue in your walk with the Lord, remember that each small step of obedience, each act of faith, each moment of surrender draws you closer to Him and shapes you more into the person He created you to be.

In these 31 days, you have learned that living out your faith is not about grand gestures or public displays but about the quiet, consistent acts of obedience that nobody else sees. It's about the private moments when you choose to trust instead of fear, to forgive instead of hold grudges, to serve when it's inconvenient, and to pray when it feels like your prayers are hitting the ceiling. Those moments are the true test of your faith, and they are where the most profound growth happens. God sees those moments, and He honors them. Your walk with the Lord is a marathon, not a sprint, and the strength to continue comes from "I am the vine, ye *are* the branches: He that abideth in me, and I in him, the same bringeth forth much fruit: for without me ye can do nothing."(John 15:5). The verbs of Scripture—those calls to action—will keep you rooted in Christ, giving you the strength and grace to persevere.

One of the most important lessons from this journey is that you are not walking alone. Throughout these 31 days, you have been reminded that God is with you every step of the way. When He calls you to come to Him, to follow Him, to trust Him, He is walking beside you, offering His guidance, comfort, and strength. His presence is what makes bold biblical action possible. The Holy Spirit empowers you to live out these commands, to answer the call, and to keep moving forward even when the road is hard. You are never alone in this journey. Deuteronomy 31:6 states "Be strong and of a good courage, fear not, nor be afraid of them: for the LORD thy God, he *it is* that doth go with thee; he will not fail thee, nor forsake thee." God's promise to never leave or forsake you is the foundation of your faith, and it is what enables you to live a life of bold action.

As you continue to walk with the Lord beyond these 31 days, remember that you are part of a larger story. Your faith is not just about your individual journey but about being part of the body of Christ. You are called to live in community, to encourage others, to serve those in need, and to speak the truth of the gospel to those who have not yet heard. Your bold biblical actions ripple out, affecting not only your own life but the lives of those around you. You are a light in a dark world, and as you continue to live, love, forgive, give thanks, and serve, you are shining the light of Christ to those who desperately need to see it.

So, what now? The call to bold biblical action does not end here. It is ongoing, and it will require daily commitment, faith, and reliance on God's grace. The verbs you have studied over these 31 days are not simply suggestions—they are the blueprint for a life lived for Christ. As you continue in your walk with the Lord, let these verbs guide you, challenge you, and inspire you to keep moving forward in faith. Continue to pray, to seek, to rejoice, and to trust. Continue to love with the love of Christ, to forgive as you have been forgiven, and to serve as Christ served. Continue to speak the truth in love and to give thanks in every circumstance. Most importantly, continue to answer the call.

The journey of faith is lifelong, but it is also deeply rewarding. As you continue to walk with the Lord, you will see His faithfulness in ways you never imagined. You will experience His peace, His joy, and His grace in deeper and more profound ways. You will grow in your understanding of His love for you and your purpose in His kingdom. And as you live out these bold biblical actions day by day, you will become more like Christ—reflecting His love, His compassion, and His truth to a world that desperately needs Him. The call to bold biblical action is not easy, but it is worth it. So, take what you have learned in these 31 days and continue to answer the call with faith, courage, and unwavering trust in the God who walks with you every step of the way.

Don't miss out!

Visit the website below and you can sign up to receive emails whenever Joshua Rhoades publishes a new book. There's no charge and no obligation.

https://books2read.com/r/B-A-AJLBB-VWICF

BOOKS 2 READ

Connecting independent readers to independent writers.

Did you love *Answer The Call - 31 Days of Biblical Action*? Then you should read *A Christmas Journey of Faith*[1] by Joshua Rhoades!

[2]

In "A Christmas Journey of Faith", join four friends—Jake, Emma, Max, and Maya—on a thrilling time-travel adventure. When they discover a mysterious time machine hidden in an old shed, they embark on an incredible journey that takes them over 2,000 years into the past to witness the most important event in history: the birth of Jesus Christ. But this journey isn't just about seeing the past—it's about learning timeless lessons of faith, trust, and courage.

As they travel back to the time of Mary and Joseph, the friends witness the Christmas story unfold. From the angel Gabriel's visit to Mary to the long journey to Bethlehem and the miraculous birth of Jesus in a humble stable, they find themselves in the heart of the greatest miracle. They stand in awe as the shepherds receive the good news from the angels, follow the star with the wise men, and learn how Mary and Joseph trusted God's plan, even when it was difficult.

---

1. https://books2read.com/u/bWA9Qz

2. https://books2read.com/u/bWA9Qz

Each step of their journey shows how faith in God can guide us through life's challenges. The friends learn that Christmas isn't about presents or decorations, but about the gift of Jesus, who came to bring peace, love, and hope to the world. As they experience these incredible events, they realize that God's love and salvation are for everyone—rich or poor, young or old.

"A Christmas Journey of Faith" is a heartwarming story that reminds readers of all ages to trust God's plan and embrace the true meaning of Christmas. Through the eyes of Jake, Emma, Max, and Maya, readers will be inspired to live out the message of salvation and faith that Jesus brought to the world.